"An important and beautifully visual affirmation that cultures throughout the ancient world always built their most impressive temples at locations whose landscapes held special significance and high energy. These sacred sites remain active, and Judy Hall offers techniques to connect the aspirant/pilgrim to their original purposes."

—**ROBIN HEATH,** *landscape researcher and author of* Stonehenge *(Wooden Books) and* Bluestone Magic *(Bluestone Press)*

"What a sublime gift to gaze into this beautifully written and prepared book. I adore the marriage of writing and photographs that celebrate the mineral kingdom and sacred sites. Crystals and Sacred Sites *opens up a whole new field of crystalline possibilities that I for one will carry with me on my travels"*

—**MICHAEL EASTWOOD,** *author of the* Crystal Oversoul Attunements, *published by Findhorn Press, 2011*

"Judy Hall is one of my favorite metaphysical authors. What I love about Judy is that she is always doing new research and is never willing to sit on her laurels. She brings us new information that is always enlightening, helpful, and encouraging. She is one of the truly humble people writing today which is a rare trait, indeed. It is because of this humility that her vast knowledge of meta-physical healing can spring forth from her cauldron of experience."

—**JOHN VAN REES, SNR.,** *Owner www.exquisitecrystals.com*

*This one is for my daughter, Jeni, with love
and thanks for her magical photographic skills.*

© 2012 Fair Winds Press
Text © 2012 Judy Hall

First published in the USA in 2012 by
Fair Winds Press, a member of
Quayside Publishing Group
100 Cummings Center
Suite 406-L
Beverly, MA 01915-6101
www.fairwindspress.com

16 15 14 13 12   1 2 3 4 5

ISBN: 978-1-59233-522-0

Digital edition published in 2012
eISBN-13: 978-1-61058-626-9

Library of Congress Cataloging-in-Publication Data
Hall, Judy, 1943-
 Crystals and sacred sites: use crystals to access the power of sacred
landscapes for personal transformation / Judy Hall.
     p. cm.
 Includes bibliographical references and index.
 ISBN 978-1-59233-522-0
 1. Crystals--Psychic aspects. 2. Sacred space. I. Title.
 BF1442.C78H345 2012
 133'.2548--dc23

                              2012020357

Book design by Kathie Alexander
Developmental Editor: Skye Alexander
Cover image: Visuals Unlimited, Inc. / Victor Habbick
Crystals and stones photography by John Van Rees, Jnr., www.exquisitecrystals.com

Printed and bound in China

*No medical claims are made for the stones in this book, and the information given is not intended to act as a
substitute for medical treatment. Healing means bringing mind, body, and spirit into balance and facilitating
evolution for the soul; it does not imply a cure.*

CRYSTALS
AND
SACRED SITES

USE CRYSTALS TO ACCESS THE POWER OF SACRED LANDSCAPES FOR PERSONAL AND PLANETARY TRANSFORMATION

JUDY HALL

AUTHOR OF THE INTERNATIONAL BESTSELLER *THE CRYSTAL BIBLE*

FAIR WINDS
PRESS
BEVERLY, MASSACHUSETTS

Contents

Introduction

CRYSTALS
AND
SACRED
LANDSCAPES

"'Tis, but I cannot name it, 'tis the sense
Of majesty, and beauty, and repose
A blended holiness of earth and sky."

—William Wordsworth, poet

Sacred tourism—traveling to sacred sites around the world—is becoming increasingly popular. More than 300,000 tourists trek to Peru's Machu Picchu each year, and 35,000 visit Stonehenge on the summer solstice alone. Not everyone, however, can travel to locations that may be in inhospitable places. Fortunately, you don't need to physically travel to a site to experience its benefits. You can journey there in your imagination, using crystals to guide you. This book shows you how.

The energy present at sacred sites is incredibly alive and highly responsive to interaction. It literally plugs you into the numinous: an enormous energy grid that encompasses your body and soul, the planet, and the cosmos. Once connected, this energy stays with you no matter where you go. It expands your awareness and heightens your sensitivity, providing healing and catalyzing your spirituality. In his foreword to *100 Journeys for the Spirit*, Pico Iyer, a close companion of the Dalai Lama for thirty years, expresses his experience this way:

"Certain places can so shock or humble us that they take us to places inside ourselves, of terror or wonder or the confounding mixture of them both, that we never see amidst the hourly distractions and clutter of home. They slap us awake, and into a recognition of who we might be in our deepest moments. I will never forget walking out onto the terrace of my broken guesthouse in Lhasa, in 1985, and seeing the Potala Palace above what was then just a cluster of traditional whitewashed Tibetan houses, its thousand windows seeming to watch over us. I will never forget, too, visiting the Church of the Holy Sepulchre in Jerusalem two years ago and feeling, whether I wanted to or not, all the prayers, hopes, and complications that people had brought to it. The place is as dark, irregular, and everyday as the fights it houses—as worldly and human as the Potala seems the opposite—and yet the very fact that so many millions have come for centuries to pray and sob among its flickering candles ensures that many more will do so, even if, like me, they're not Christian or Buddhist or anything. Places have charisma, in short, much as people do."

Crystals serve as keys that open portals to numinous spots on our planet, allowing you to access their power. (I use the term *crystals* to mean precious and semiprecious stones, rocks, and minerals that have a crystalline structure at their hearts and *tektites* or other stones, that don't.) This book takes you on a journey around the globe, a sinuous path following the dragon lines and crystal bones that underpin our world. With the assistance of crystal tools, you access this numinous grid and open the limitless possibilities of your imagination.

I invite you to join me on this journey into sanctity. Your "crystal travel agent," along with the information in this book, assist you in your journey of the imagination to the sacred sites of your choice.

Part One

Understanding
Sacred Landscapes

Chapter I

HOW LANDSCAPES AFFECT US

*"A journey of the spirit only starts with somewhere wondrous.
It continues wherever we are, through the doors that wonder has opened."*

—*Pico Iyer,* 100 Journeys for the Spirit

*H*aving lived in an ancient part of Dorset, England, for more than a quarter century, I intimately understand how a landscape imbued with sanctity affects us. My home is on the outermost edge of the Earth's heart chakra, which stretches from Glastonbury in Somerset to Shaftesbury in Dorset. To the west, I am bounded by the Dorset Cursus, the oldest ritual way in England. To my east, lie Knowlton Henges, three Chalk bank-and-ditch circles that once held an Ironstone circle. Dominated by the ruins of an ancient church, this site's guardian yew trees are almost 2,000 years old, offshoots of much older trees. The site affects me deeply. It is my inspiration and my solace.

Knowlton Henge and Barrow Complex, Dorset, England

Psychogeology

Knowlton provides a viewing platform for a skyscape of eclipses and other celestial events. The midsummer sunset appears, disappears, and reappears as it rolls down a fold in the surrounding hills. I have spent many nights there watching the sky with awe and wonder, feeling a sense of the numinous all around me. This is how ancient people would have viewed the celestial dome, plotting the changing cycles of seasons and celestial events against its eternal, slowly revolving astronomical background.

Knowlton perches between two geologies: Chalk and Greensand. It is a liminal space, a "thin place" that joins the known with the unknown, transcendent with incarnated. The site brings together two of my pas-sions—landscape archaeology and archaeoastronomy—and unites them with a third: crystals. Around Knowl-ton are burial mounds with carefully crafted pieces of Flint interred within them. It would be difficult not to be affected by the sheer antiquity of my landscape. When I travel, I carry a small piece of local Flint with me, because it holds the essence of my homeland.

Living on Chalk, as I do, is an energetic experience like no other. Chalk is a fluid medium, composed of organisms that once lived at the bottom of the sea. Dorset's Chalk is interwoven with Flint, a portal stone whose energetic properties convey me between the material and spiritual worlds. It suits my metaphysical self and heightens my intuition—so different from the claggy, clay-capped hill only a few miles away on which I briefly alighted ten years ago, and where my metaphysical

When man went to the Moon, he brought back a rock.

awareness was strangely dulled. And different, too, from the soul-scouring, focused harshness of Cornish Granite with its strong geomagnetic resonance that made me feel strangely melancholy; and from the abrasive qualities of Sandstone at the other end of Dorset that sharpened my perceptions to a razor's edge but made it difficult for me to relax.

Psychogeology states that our minds are shaped by the landscape around us. Few of us stop to think when choosing a home that the geology on which it sits, or the material from which the house is formed, may deeply impact our energetic or cognitive functioning.

But our ancestors were aware. Attuned to the nuances of the landscape and its underlying geology, they knew how to harness and manipulate natural forces in the landscape to affect human behavior. That's why they sited their sacred places where they did—not for easy accessibility, but because the land itself was special, numinous, powerful, and divine.

Atmospheric conditions, the intensity of sunlight, barometric and temperature variations profoundly affect our physiological and psychological functioning. And, although we may be less cognizant of it, we are influenced deeply by the geology of the landscape, as well as by geophysical and celestial phenomena. Some rocks are highly geomagnetic, some retain water, and others allow water to pass through rapidly. Concentrations of mineral ore, geomagnetism, volcanic activity, and subsurface water affect us.

Knowing why a sacred site is located where it is, and understanding the history and myths that surround the place, help you to immerse yourself in its energies and the possibilities it offers you. So does recognizing why ancient peoples chose these incredible sites for their rites, rituals, and shamanic workings.

The Geology of the Numinous

Rocks profoundly affect those who interact with them. During the *Apollo 15* landing on the Moon, astronaut Jim Irwin found a 4.15-billion-year-old Genesis Rock he described as "perched like an outstretched hand on a rocky pulpit." At that moment, Irwin states, he heard the voice of God in his ear. The sparkling white, Anorthosite crystalline rock is almost as old as our solar system and far older than any rock on Earth. When Irwin returned to Earth, he became a "Goodwill Ambassador for the Prince of Peace." He frequently commented that his experiences in space had made the presence of God utterly real to him.

Crystals literally underpin our world. Indeed, many sacred sites, such as Peru's Machu Picchu and Tibet's Mount Kailash, are rumored to have secret crystal caverns at their hearts. Rocks with a high Quartz content—such as Granite, Sandstone, and Quartzite—or with a high metallic content of iron, copper, silver, gold, or rutile, form a giant electrical conducting system, amplifying natural Earth energies passing through them.

Sites such as Lourdes in France feature natural healing water. Lourdes has high concentrations of a rare metal, germanium, within its rocks. An excellent energy conductor, germanium has been shown to be antiviral and antibacterial, and to stimulate the production of T cells, the body's natural immune system. Lourdes was an ancient healing site long before Saint Bernadette's visions of the Virgin Mary made it famous in the nineteenth century.

Genesis Rock found on the Moon.

Scientists are finding that the geological underpinnings of sacred sites contribute to mind and mood alteration. Geochemical trace elements such as copper, zinc, and lithium in the environment all play a part. Lithium, for example, has calming properties. Tectonic plate movements create "transient, bizarre, and unusual behaviors." In ancient Greece, an oracular Temple of Apollo at Delphi sat on rock saturated with petrochemical fumes. The presence of these fumes caused the priestesses who prophesied at this site to go into altered states of consciousness as happened to me there and at Dodona, both oracular sites.

Standing in a cave high on Patmos, Greece, where Saint John the Divine is reputed to have written the biblical book of Revelation, I knew how that prophetic book came into being. The cave is redolent with nightmarish, hallucinogenic visions. I understood Revelation while I was there, but my awareness faded once I returned to sea level. Long before the monastery of Saint John the Divine was built, a temple stood on top of the mountain. Patmos is, and always has been, a sacred island.

Many sacred sites grew up because of unique geological features—crystalline rocks, naturally strong geomagnetism, or simulacra (rocks that resemble a human face or an animal). But sacred places weren't chosen merely for aesthetics; they were an integral part of ancient cos-

Stones were often chosen for the faces depicted in the rock.

mology. These sites are multiexperiential and multilay-ered, held within the landscape and integral to it. They evolved over thousands of years, sometimes changing their focus while maintaining their sanctity.

A number of the world's most numinous sites are at tectonic plate junctions or on the joining point of two distinct geologies, creating a liminal space—a portal be-tween worlds. Tectonic plate junctions are where earth-quakes occur. The Earth is continually moving due to one plate slipping against or over another. This is quite literally where you feel the Earth move, which must have reinforced the idea that the planet was a living entity, as did volcanoes that appeared to exhale fiery breath. Similarly, changes in geology signaled a change in the body of Mother Earth as the energy moved

through the distinctive rocks in diverse ways, creating an energetic hiatus that sensitive people can feel. For instance, where fluid energy running through Chalk abuts Greenstone a line of swirling geomagnetic cur-rents is generated, and where Flint seams run through the Chalk the energy is held as though in a container.

CAPTURING POWER

Early in the Christian era, Pope Gregory told his mis-sionaries to site their churches on ancient pagan sites so as to assume the power therein. Saint Michael's Church atop Glastonbury Tor, sited in an ancient sacred landscape, pinned down the dragon power of the Tor. Mayan sites are located on much earlier Meso-american temples. It has always been so.

Chapter 2

USING CRYSTALS
TO CONNECT WITH
SACRED SITES

"In the ancient landscape everything is connected, nothing is in violation."
—Peter Knight, Megalithomania Conference 2011

---

*T*his book explores the interconnections between landscape, geology, crystals, and power. But, with a few exceptions, it does not feature crystals or rocks actually found at sacred sites. Rather, it uses crystals that resonate with specific sites. That is, the crystals invoke the healing, consciousness-expanding, divine connection and other qualities of the site.

Crystal Collection

Many people instinctively pick up stones as keepsakes. However, this may have dire consequences. The visitor site at Hawaii Volcanoes National Park has a huge store of letters from people around the world who have returned stones because removing them brought those people "bad luck." This is especially so if you haven't asked permission to enter a site or a site hasn't offered up a stone to you.

This book shows you how to choose and use crystals to connect with the geology of particular sacred sites. You needn't take a stone away or even visit a site physically to experience its majesty. That's the magic of crystals and the power of the photography in this book!

CRYSTAL COMMUNICATION

Fortunately, all crystals of the same type communicate with each other—and with you—regardless of their present location or where they were sourced. Consequently, you can use this characteristic to tune into the crystals themselves and to the landscape(s) with which they are aligned. You learn how to do this and how to meet the crystal oversouls (sentient beings who share a unified consciousness) a little later in this book.

Sound serves as another type of crystal communication. Ancient people utilized lithophones (percussive rocks) that rang like a drum when struck or sounded like a flute when the wind blew through them. Stalactites were "rung" when people still lived in caves—the pure bell-like sound must have seemed magical indeed. At one lithophonic site in Russia, natural stone drum tones are magnified by the surrounding lake, so that the sound is heard many kilometers away.

Sacred Earth Energies

Sacred sites—places of awe, mystery, and wonder—are located where they are because of the combination of geological, aesthetic, geodesic, geomagnetic, symbolic, astronomical, mythological, and shamanic factors operating in the landscape according to the belief systems of the people who constructed these sites. Crystals form an integral part of sacred geography because they share these qualities.

All of the world's numinous places have deities, legends, and traditions attached to them. Some of these may still be obtained from oral or written histories; others can only be guessed at or accessed by expanded consciousness. Yet others are being created now. This book explores the geomythological landscape—crystal-deity associations, drawing on both historical and modern connections. You'll find them discussed in Part 2 along with the individual stones. The New Age and Ascension movements assign chakra and angelic connections to power places and vortex sites. I examine these locales, as well as traditional and new sacred sites.

EARTH ENERGY DISRUPTION AND DESECRATION

Sacred sites have inherently strong Earth energies created by geophysics, ley lines, underground water, telluric or dragon currents, and the like. (We'll discuss these under the different sites.) Indigenous people, who treat their landscapes with great respect, are aware of how Earth energies can be disrupted as described in this communication from Antonio Velasco about the challenges of mining a unique Quartz combination:

> *"The Earth gives us the fruit and [it] should only be collected when ripe. [In local belief] it is prohibited to cut any roots of the earth. In the lake of the quartz, streams of energy are subdivided. Each 'arm' ends in five fingers and each finger gives a different material. When any of these small deposits are accidentally cut by construction of a road or any other activity, miners repair this stretch by placing the crystals orientated in the right way to regenerate the energy flow."*

John Van Rees of Exquisite Crystals describes on his website how his company's Nepalese Quartz is obtained, explaining how important it is to local people to approach crystals connected with sacred sites with awe and honor.

> *"These crystal wonders are hand-harvested from a family-owned mine in the Himalayan Mountains of Nepal. Before the family can even consider crystal harvesting, they must ask permission of the mountain. If the mountain says 'No' then they freely release the idea. If the mountain says 'Yes' then they offer thanks and rituals and begin the arduous three-day bus ride to the mine.*

Once at the mountain, they must climb extremely carefully (with packs) on primitive paths and bridges. When they find the place where the mountain is offering her stones to them, they gently harvest them with small hand-held hammers.

Then they kindly wrap each crystal to preserve every single, precious point. It requires great intent and dedication to then climb, from 10,000 feet plus, down and take the three-day bus ride back home with their treasures.

It is not the easy way to 'mine' stones. It would be 'easier' to use heavy equipment, or dynamite. However, this heart-filled way of asking the mountain, first, and then hand-gathering, is how they lovingly honor the Earth. They create sacred space where the Earth's resources are respected for the true treasures that they are.

We feel enormously grateful to be able to support this way of treating the earth and her bounty with kindness and gratitude. When we share these crystals with you, we share that kindness and honoring with you. It is literally imbued in every stone. We know that some of their brightness directly comes from the clear compassion offered them. It is a way of life that creates more life."

www.exquisitecrystals.com

Fortunately, it is not necessary to travel to Nepal—nor to any of the world's sacred places—to connect with its energy. You can attune yourself through meditation and guided visualization journeys, holding a crystal that links you with the site's energy and intention.

The Power of Landscape

The following quotation comes from a work of fiction, but it has the ring of authentic experience behind it. It shows the power that landscape has on us, what ancient humans might have felt as they stood in numinous places, and what we can feel today. In this case, the landscape described is a patch of desert.

A barren desert can provoke a sacred experience.

"He felt an odd tingle of anticipation, as if he were on the verge of what he had been waiting for, his revelation, his epiphany. Someone had once told him that there were places you could go that would change you . . .

For so long now he had been struggling in the dark, and in that desert night when the motel's blinking red neon was nothing but a dot on the horizon, he found an epiphany of a kind . . . when it came it was nothing more than a simple, fleeting ripple of happiness that went through him as a light, cool breeze might brush one's skin on a hot day . . . but he knew that he would be OK, that he was OK, that he could deal with things. His problems didn't matter in the midst of the desert night—the myriad stars above and grains of sand under his feet . . . He was a long, long way from home, but, oddly enough, he didn't feel so far away at that moment."

Peter Robinson, Bad Boy

Peter Robinson's graphic description reminds us that it is in the small things that we find sacred connection. That tiny "ripple of happiness" changes the course of a life. Although such experiences may seem outside of time, they have a profound effect on the present moment. They are part of ancient cosmology: a holistic paradigm that takes spirituality, astronomy, mythology, and theology and creates an integrated worldview in which gods speak, places empower or overawe, and the world is forever changed in one moment.

THE POWER OF CEREMONY

The ceremonies, rituals, and journeys in this book have been created to act as keys to sacred power. They are not tied to any specific native tradition, but honor them all in spirit rather than in authentic practice. If you have training in or ancestral knowledge of a particular tradition, you can add to the power by inputting your own awareness.

A SENSE OF THE SACRED

The word *sacred* comes from the Latin word for "set aside." It can be applied to anything that is venerated or treated with awe, be it a place, a person, or an object. Closely connected is the word *numinous*, meaning the "mysterious power of the divine." Today, we often think of the divine as something other, a different reality. But in ancient times, the gods and goddesses interpenetrated everything, although their activities were often regarded as supernatural rather than part of everyday reality.

Sacred sites bring these ideas together. Such sites are invariably places of great power and in antiquity were, for the most part, frequented by those who mediated with the deities on behalf of the people. Through virtue of their long use, ancient sites—even those now abandoned—are imbued with palpable power. The website www.sacredsites.com describes it as: "Similar to the power of a magnet, the power of a numinous site is an invisible field of energy permeating the area of the sacred site." It is as though the very stones and/or the landscape are impregnated with power. You feel, touch, even taste it. You know when you are stepping into a numinous landscape. The air tingles or seems preternaturally still. The land beneath your feet has a special quality. You literally walk on sacred ground.

Sacred Site Protocol

When visiting an actual site, always ask permission of the site's spirit guardian before entering. Respect local customs and dress appropriately. It is permissible to make an offering, but don't leave "new age litter" behind you. Sites are becoming increasingly polluted with ribbons, candle wax, and decaying offerings that add nothing to the energy of a site. Do not grid or plant crystals in the earth unless requested to do so by the highest guidance, as doing so can interfere with the energy of the Earth's meridian grid surrounding the site. Take away nothing that is not freely offered.

Sacred litter is unsightly and does not enhance the energy of a site.

Chapter 3

A
LANDSCAPE
SET IN STONE

"The nature of that landscape is in the rocks as much as in anything else out there—maybe more so. Their age, their presence, is something that controls one's mind and sets one's mood."
—Richard Allen, www.psychogeology.com

A site possesses an inherent sacredness due to its location, geology, awesome beauty, innate power, ability to inspire visionary experiences, and so on. But sacredness also arises from the input of human beings who augment, magnify, and decorate the site to harness its natural energies. This input occurs at dual levels: the functional and the intentional. Intention, or belief, recognizes and builds on the inherent power at a location and ensures this awareness stays in the folk memory. The functional side arises from the material used to build or shape a site, whether the site is natural or man made. The material most frequently used for this augmentation of the divine is stone.

Building with Stone and Crystal

In early cultures where houses were built of mud, brick, and straw, people went to enormous trouble to enhance or shape rock for divine purposes or to build whole structures in stone. For aeons, people have decorated their sacred sites with crystals or mineral pigments. Crystals and rocks were deemed to have supernatural powers that catalyzed spiritual development, induced trance states and visionary experiences, and formed a fitting home for the deities.

A high ratio of Quartz allows rocks to create and convey electromagnetic currents. Granite has natural radioactivity, and Granite landscapes tend to be wild and melancholy places. Geomagnetic rocks have been shown to facilitate healing. Ancient people incorporated layers of organic and inorganic matter into structures to amplify the natural power at the site. They also moved stones from one location to another to energetically connect the two places.

STONES USED AT ANCIENT SITES

- *Stones Found at the Site:* Rocks with subtle geomagnetic energies, concentrations of specific minerals, striking figurations, or high Quartz content frequently form the geological basis for numinous places. Compasses go crazy over specific stones. These stones are known to create altered states of consciousness. In England, monuments were often delineated with brilliant white Chalk or Snow Quartz. Chalk holds moonlight. Quartz holds sunlight, although Snow (White) Quartz also soaks up moonlight. The stone's crystalline makeup actually stores light, similar to the way plants utilise sunlight for photosynthesis.

- *Stones Brought to the Site from a Distance:* Newgrange in Ireland is fronted with Quartz—tons of it—that came from 50 miles (80 km) away. That was a huge undertaking back in the Stone Age. The Preseli Bluestones at Stonehenge were transported 150 miles (241 km) from Pembrokeshire, West Wales. Aswan Granite, which contains natural radioactivity and high paramagnetic resonance, is found in temples all over Egypt.

- *A Combination of the Two:* Rocks native to an area were enhanced by specific stones transported from elsewhere. The Egyptian pyramids were faced with local Limestone, but the internal construction is of Aswan Granite. According to folk memory, the Great Pyramid was topped with a pure Quartz pyramidion. In Aztec temples, Obsidian and Agate are set into the mortar between the stones.

Virtually all sacred sites include pure Quartz or rock with high Quartz content. Quartz is a storehouse for energy. It vibrates at a very specific rate. When struck or compressed, it creates an electrical discharge that is visible in the dark. When light shines through it, refraction produces a rainbow. Quartz also transmits sound (think of early crystal radio sets). To the ancients, it must have seemed magical indeed.

Parts of our brains, in particular the temporal lobe, are receptive to crystal power and to magnetic energies. Tradition says certain stones were used as pillows to induce dreams, visions, altered states of consciousness, and healings. Ancient humans may have had a particularly well-developed sensitivity to electromagnetic and other natural energies and used these energies to enhance their spiritual experiences and to navigate their landscape.

Crystal Oversouls

For thousands of years crystals, were considered sentient beings and treated with the awe and respect due to incarnated gods. Ancient people believed stones could communicate because they were alive. Each type of crystal shared a unified consciousness, an awareness of being one spirit widely scattered across a large area, and yet intimately connected. Today, that spirit is known as a crystal oversoul. In his card pack the *Crystal Oversoul Attunements*, Michael Eastwood explains it this way: "Crystal oversouls are part of the fabric of cosmic creation . . . the collective soul that all individual crystals in its field will identify and communicate with."

Time and space have no effect on crystal consciousness. The unified resonance between crystals of the same type, no matter where they may be situated, enables us to use crystals from other sources to connect to a specific sacred site. Similar crystals may be embedded in the bedrock at a site. Learning to attune to the crystal oversouls is a simple process of focusing your attention and intention.

The mandala to the right is the energy pattern of the Lapis Lazuli oversoul. The ancient Egyptians believed Lapis Lazuli to be the embodiment of Ra, the Sun god. The stone was transported thousands of miles from Afghanistan and used to craft sacred objects.

Mandala of the Lapis Lazuli oversoul

Connecting to the Crystal Oversoul

Gaze into the center of the mandala, holding a piece of Lapis Lazuli if you have one. Feel your awareness being lifted up, transported into the energy field of the Lapis Lazuli oversoul. Feel how it expands your awareness, so you communicate with Lapis wherever it may be. Listen to the crystal's message.

When you have completed your attunement to the oversoul, open your eyes to break off contact. Settle your awareness back into your body, stand, and be aware of the contact you make to the Earth.

You can attune to other oversouls by holding the appropriate crystal and expanding your awareness in the same manner.

Chapter 4

HOW TO USE THIS BOOK

"His story is a living string of ceremonies to help heal hearts, align energies, right ancient imbalances, and balance the living Earth's Unity Consciousness Grid —in short to increase our awareness of the indivisibility of life in the universe. We are all—rocks and people and interdimensional beings—one!"

—Serpent of Light: Beyond 2012

*H*ave you ever wanted to visit a sacred site but didn't have the means to travel there? Now you can, without leaving the comfort of your home. The crystals and accompanying exercises in this book act as keys that enable you to connect with a sacred site and harness that site's energy.

Crystals and the Numinous

Crystals and the numinous have a natural interaction that people have drawn on for millennia. Part of Australian Aboriginal initiation rituals involved swallowing Quartz and driving Quartz crystals into the body to store power. You won't need to go that far—all you need do is hold Quartz or other crystals to activate power in yourself. In this way, you draw power from a sacred site for healing, to expand your awareness, catalyze your spirituality, connect to the ancestors, or speak to your or the site's deity. An experiential connection raises your consciousness and allows you to reach the dimensions normally reserved for the ancestors or the deities.

The stones presented in Part 2 of this book have been specially chosen because they possess an energetic resonance with the sacred sites with which they are paired.

ACCESSING SACRED SITES VIA CRYSTALS

Select a site that has a particular resonance for you. This may be through ancestral or past-life links, or cultural or belief connections. Or, you may feel attracted to the site and wish to know more about it. Look through the illustrations in this book. They may give you a jolt, the kind that says, "I'm here, waiting." When you've decided which site attracts you most, read the description and then establish your energetic connection. Before connecting to the crystal, you could take an Internet tour of a site, courtesy of Google Earth and the Megalithic Portal (www.megalithic.co.uk), which allows you to view a sacred site anywhere in the world.

You may already have one of the crystals associated with the site you want to explore, but alternative crystals are suggested—work with the one that resonates best with your personal energies.

USING THE JOURNEYS, CEREMONIES, AND MEDITATIONS

Once you've cleansed and awakened your crystal (see page 24), gather everything you need, switch off your phone, ensure you will not be disturbed, and find a quiet place to settle down. Hold the crystal and follow the instructions provided for the site you've chosen—they can be recorded if the journey or meditation is a long one. Remember to leave appropriate pauses.

Real people's experiences are included in some site descriptions. These show how a place might affect you and what to expect. But, as with all things crystal, there is no one right way to access these sites or to work with the stones associated with them. You will have your own, unique experience, one that is exactly right for you, and it may evolve over time.

It is best to approach the journey with no preconceptions and no expectations other than connecting to the energy of the site for your highest good. This leaves room for serendipity. You let the divine manifest in whatever form is appropriate for you. Approaching the journey in a spirit of adventure and open-mindedness allows the stone and the site to unfold their mysteries. Leave behind your desire for results, and let the journey open in the way that modern-day geomancer Barry Brailsford set off on his own shamanic landscape journey:

> *"Letting go, accepting without understanding, stepping out without knowing the final destination, recognising and listening to a voice within that was growing strong with the trusting."*

> Song of the Stone

This is what makes such a journey magical. It allows you to uniquely experience the sites and the stones. In other words, to find insights and connections that are truly your own.

Keeping Your Crystals Sacred

Crystals need to be awakened and purified before use and, because they rapidly draw off energy from their surroundings, they need frequent purifying to maintain their power (see below). Treat your crystals with respect and work with them in partnership. They'll repay you with years of devoted service. Treat them badly or misuse them, and their power may turn against you. They are, after all, magical, sentient beings.

Crystals work by cooperating with you to focus and manifest your intention. Be clear about why you are working with the crystal and ensure that you are working for the highest good. Misuse of crystal power inevitably rebounds. Like humans, crystals can become exhausted, so reempower them regularly.

CHOOSING YOUR CRYSTALS

Each of the sacred sites in this book is paired with a crystal associated with the site. Alternative crystals are suggested in case you have difficulty obtaining specific crystals, although virtually all these stones are available on the Internet (see Resources). If you already have the primary crystal in your own collection, or one of the alternatives, this will work well for you. If you don't have the appropriate crystal, visit a crystal shop and see what jumps out at you, or browse the Internet. Or, simply use the power of the crystal illustration as this holds the magical presence of the crystal. You'll soon find what you seek.

PURIFYING YOUR CRYSTALS

Crystals pick up energy from anyone who handles them as well as from the environment, so they need cleansing before and after drawing off negative energy. Purify crystals by holding them under running water—so long as they won't dissolve or fragment in the process. You can also smudge a crystal by holding it in incense smoke or leaving it overnight in uncooked brown rice.

Candle flames can be cleansing for crystals.

Put the crystal in sunlight or moonlight to charge it (white crystals prefer moonlight, although Quartz is happy with either). Alternatively, use one of the ready-made crystal cleansers and reenergizers listed in the Resources section of this book.

AWAKENING YOUR CRYSTAL

To awaken its energy, hold the purified crystal in your hands, focus your attention on it, and say

"I dedicate this crystal to the highest good of all and ask that its power be activated now to work in harmony with my own will and focused intention."

To deactivate the crystal, cleanse it and then hold the crystal as you say

"I thank this crystal for its power, which is no longer needed at this time. I ask that its power be closed until reactivated."

Then place it in a bag, box, or drawer until you require its assistance again.

The Chalice Well, Glastonbury, flower-dressed for the spring equinox. ▶

Part Two

Sacred Sites and Their Corresponding Crystals

Chapter 5

THE HOME OF THE STONE PEOPLE

— INUKSUK AT THE CIRCUMPOLAR REGIONS —

"Inuit nature religion builds on 'inua,' which means strength. Nature is living, strong, powerful and full of secrets. Everything—animals and natural phenomenon—have a special life force, an inner energy and power. And each inua has its own individual characteristics."

—www.greenland.com

SACRED SITES
INUKSUK AT THE CIRCUMPOLAR REGIONS, NORTHERN CANADA, THE ARCTIC CIRCLE 66°33' N AND KANDAHAR, AFGHANISTAN 1°37' N 65°43' E

CORRESPONDING CRYSTAL
SERPENTINE

Stone figures dominate the Arctic landscape. The Inuit erected Inuksuk and other stone objects to mark a significant place, give directions, provide protection, and as objects of veneration. Rather than being one site, Nunatsiaq is the traditional land of the Inuit and includes the snowy "wastelands" above the Arctic Circle. But this land was also known as "the bountiful and beautiful" because, for more than 5,000 years, it provided the Inuit and those who came before them with plentiful food and shelter.

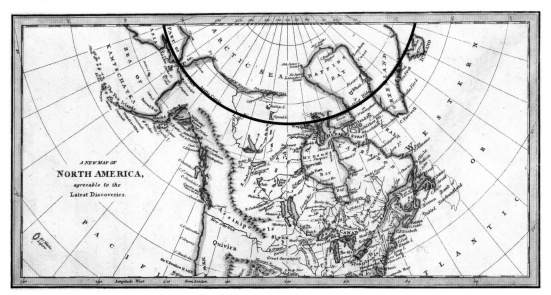

Circumpolar Regions

What these sites offer you

- Connection to inua, strength, or the life force
- Survival skills in an alien landscape
- Environmental support to the planet
- A memorial to the fallen and a way to help the spirit home

Crystal Connections

Amazing crystals are found inside the Arctic Circle. Shamanic Serpentine is everywhere. Gentle Tugtupite is found only in Greenland, and Nuummite—the ancient sorcerers' stone and perhaps the oldest crystal on the planet—only in the circumpolar regions. Natural egg-shaped white Quartz has a special place in Inuit lore. Exquisite Greenland gems have high vibrations that facilitate spiritual evolution, returning us to oneness. Their loving energy teaches us to once more respect and honor the Earth and everything in and on it. The Inuit erect Inuksuk from stones such as local Granite. They also carve smaller ones from Serpentine, Jade, Marble, and other stones.

Nunatsiaq: The Land That Remains in the Heart

In *Tukiliit: The Stone People Who Live in the Wind*, Norman Hallendy writes that the Inuit believed natural features, or ujaraqtalik, had supernatural powers, and nunaupmannia, round white stones that resemble goose eggs, were the eggs from which sacred white caribou were born. The people placed beautiful white Quartz, or patiujaq, on graves to assist the deceased's inua (life force) as he or she traveled through the sky.

The Inuit constructed Inuksuk in several forms:

- **innunguaq** were built in the likeness of a person.

- **sakkabluniit** were objects imbued with spiritual power.

- **angakkurvik** marked sites of shamanic initiation, and a **tupqujaq** created the doorway through which the shaman passed into the spirit world;

- A **kattaq**, formed by two stacks of stones, marked the gateway to a ritual site;

- A **tunillarvik** was a single stone that provided protection for those who offered it gifts.

The stone messengers on the landscape offered keys to living here successfully. They pointed out directions, marked sacred sites and plentiful hunting locations, and signified the enormous power of the landscape.

The Shaman's Stone: Serpentine

Serpentine is one of the few crystals collected above the Arctic Circle. Throughout the world, it has long been used to navigate safely through the unseen worlds and, with its snakelike appearance, is a symbol of spiritual resurrection.

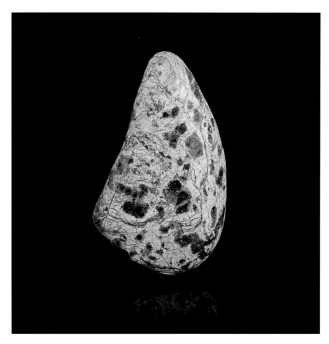

Serpentine

SERPENTINE'S PROPERTIES

Serpentine lends you the cunning of a serpent when traveling in the Underworld for soul-retrieval purposes. It powers the shaman's flight and invokes contact with other worlds, activating shapeshifting and rebirth. Serpentine helps you recognize the soul's wisdom and understand the effect your past lives have on the present. The stone awakens kundalini power. Kundalini is a magical, tantric blending of masculine and feminine sexual currents, a subtle electromagnetic energy that flashes through the chakras and ignites the flame of spiritual love, bringing union with the divine. Having passed from the base chakra up to the crown, it curls down to lie below the navel in the dantien, blending carnal desire and expanded awareness of your own power into a potent creative force. Serpentine integrates the divine into everyday life, uniting the spiritual will with the personal, creating an enlightened, empowered human being.

◀ A stone Inuksuk walks the land.

Serpentine Inuksuk carved by Luke Nakoolak.

SERPENTINE'S HEALING PROPERTIES

Serpentine has long been prized for its healing virtue. Controlling the flow of insulin within the body and regulating the pancreas, traditionally it eliminates parasites and treats pain.

Ritual: Building an Inuksuk

Create a simple Inuksuk by stacking several stones on top of each other. As you build the figure, focus your attention on the power of inua so that it imbues your sculpture. If you are building it as a memorial to one of the fallen, keep that person in mind as you build and ask the Inuksuk to help carry the spirit home. If you are building it to help the planet, focus your thoughts on what you can do to stop the ice caps' shrinking.

Alternative Crystals

Any of the circumpolar crystals can be used to build a Inuksuk.

Jade

Tugtupite

Nuummite

Sister Site: Kandahar, Afghanistan

Inuksuk at Kandahar Airfield.

Coming Home to Peace and Rest

In the fourth century BCE, Alexander the Great founded Kandahar. It has been fought over ever since. In 2002, the Third Battalion of Princess Patricia's Canadian Light Infantry created an Inuksuk from local slate at Kandahar Airfield, Afghanistan, to honor four of their colleagues killed by friendly fire. It has since become a memorial for all those killed or wounded in the Afghanistan campaigns. At its base, a dedication plaque reads as follows:

Inuksuk

The term inuksuk means,
"to act in the capacity of a human"

Among the many practical functions,
they were employed as hunting and navigational
aids, often showing the direction towards
a food supply or home.

In addition to their earthly functions,
certain Inuksuk had spiritual connotations
and were objects of veneration,

Often marking the threshold
of the spiritual landscape

Or in other words Sacred Ground

We hope that this place will remain
sacred and that the Spirits of our fallen comrades
will find their way home to peace and rest.

Chapter 6

THE DIAMOND IN THE WILDERNESS

— LAKE LOUISE —

*"The supreme and benevolent angelic presence of ArcAngel Michael enriche[s] the energy
of this area as a tool of the Ascension . . . The Divine presence has always been discernable here . . .
This is truly 'The magnificent,' the face of God, and it always has been."*

—James Tyberonn, www.earth-keeper.com

SACRED SITE
LAKE LOUISE, BANFF, ALBERTA,
CANADA 51°25' N 116°10' W

CORRESPONDING CRYSTAL
CANADIAN AMETHYST

Nestled in the Rocky Mountains, Lake Louise straddles the
Canada–United States border. Part of Banff National Park
since the mid-1800s, this sacred site gained a reputation in the
twenty-first century as the etheric retreat of Archangel Michael
and his complement, Faith. This beautiful lake sits in a basin
with an Amethyst core. Amethyst provides an excellent shield
during metaphysical working and is perfect for attuning to
archangels and multidimensional realities.

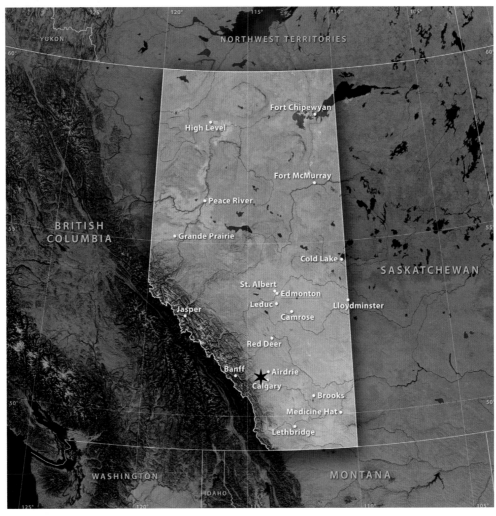

★ Lake Louise, Banff, Alberta, Canada

What this site offers you

- Spiritual peace and sanctuary for your soul
- Divine protection and teaching from your archangel of choice
- A sense of sacred guardianship in your everyday life
- A source to call upon for assistance in time of need

Crystal Connections

The Rocky Mountains, the backbone of the North American continent, have a seemingly inexhaustible supply of crystal energy and beautiful stones. The main rocks are Shale, Sandstone, Granite, Limestone, and Quartzite, and some boulders exhibit beautiful purple bands of Amethyst within them. This area was pushed up by a huge collision of tectonic plates. Rocks from such an event have powerful energies that help you adapt and survive.

Lake Louise's glacial meltwater contains a high percentage of powdered Quartz. It is suggested that this water forms a fluid crystalline battery, or as the website www.earth-keeper.com puts it, "a sacred living crystal of unmatched light and colour" that infuses the whole area with an immense and utterly unique spiritual power.

The diversity of the rocks at Lake Louise is shown in the foreground pebbles.

An Archangelic Retreat: Lake Louise

An area of pristine wilderness and awesome natural beauty, Lake Louise is protected by wings of Quartz-rich rock that amplify the divine energy at its heart. The geophysical energies have a gentle intensity, lifting burdens and harmonizing the auras of all who visit here, whether or not they are on spiritual pilgrimages.

As befits an area with volcanic activity, Banff has hot springs and, because of its height, snowcaps and permanent glaciers. Archaeological evidence dates the first human activity to 10,300 BCE. Known as Ho-run-num-nay, the Lake of the Little Fishes, it was later named Louise after Princess Louise Caroline Alberta, daughter of Queen Victoria. Today, the area is valued for its outstanding natural beauty and its spiritual emanations.

MYTHOLOGY, LEGENDS, AND LORE

According to ascension lore, each of seven archangels has a feminine complement and an etheric retreat to which your soul can withdraw for healing and teaching. These retreats are situated over geographical locations but, as they exist at a high vibration, they are accessed through meditation and expanded consciousness. In each retreat, a flame holds the essence of the spiritual quality of the archangel. Each retreat is attributed a crystal. Lake Louise is the retreat of Michael, the spiritual warrior who guides and protects.

ENERGY PATTERNS IN THE AREA

The Earth's electromagnetic grid has an etheric counterpart with a chakra system that radiates above the planet. The chakra system may be worldwide or more localized. When the two grids are in alignment, the whole area is infused with a deep sense of peace and rightness. The Earth's etheric chakra system, when in balance, naturally aligns a human being who is in contact with this subtle energy system.

THE MICHAEL VORTEX

The anchorage points for the power vortex above the Lake Louise area are three mountain peaks: Cathedral, Victoria, and Michael. This vortex channels high-vibration energy counterclockwise into three lakes feeding the Earth's electromagnetic grid so that the energy is distributed into a much wider area.

ROCKY MOUNTAIN CHAKRA SYSTEM

James Tyberonn points out that a chakra system connected to the Michael portal runs through Banff National Park, powered by the crystal-infused waters and connected by a ley. Lake Louise lies at the heart center.

- Crown chakra: Lake O'Hara
- Third eye: Emerald Lake
- Throat chakra: Lake Moraine
- Heart chakra: Lake Louise
- Solar plexus: Peyto Lake
- Sacral chakra: Brow Falls
- Base chakra: Athabasca Falls

The Archangel Retreats

Archangels	Place	Flame	Quality	Crystal
Michael and Faith	Lake Louise	Blue	Spiritual warrior	Lapis Lazuli
Jophiel and Christine	Lanzhou, China	Yellow	Cosmic wisdom	Yellow Jade
Chamuel and Charity	St. Louis, Missouri	Pink	Divine love	Rhodochrosite
Gabriel and Hope	Mount Shasta, California	White	Purity	Mount Shasta Opal
Raphael and Mary	Fatima, Portugal	Green	Healing	Fuchsite
Uriel and Aurora	Tatra Mountains, Poland	Golden	Peace and rebirth	Topaz
Zadkiel and Amethyst	Cuba	Violet Flame	Transmutation	Amethyst

Canadian Amethyst (Auralite 23)

Divine Protection: Canadian Amethyst

Amethyst has a high spiritual vibration and stimulates metaphysical abilities of all kinds. Amethyst from the Rocky Mountains is exceptionally pure. It opens the higher crown chakras, drawing in the highest guidance and inviting the presence of archangels and ascended masters. It connects you to another reality.

AMETHYST'S PROPERTIES

This calming stone deepens meditation and opens your inner sight. A strongly metaphysical crystal, it connects to multiple dimensions, opening your awareness and stimulating contact with higher beings. Amethyst is a stone of protection, particularly against attachment by discarnate spirits. It sends these spirits to the light, guided by angels.

AMETHYST'S HEALING POWER

An effective destressor, this stone traditionally guarded against drunkenness and poison. It harmonizes the brain's hemispheres and supports the immune, endo-crine, and nervous systems. A useful Earth healer, it can be gridded in an area of disharmony or instability, either at the physical site or on a map.

CONNECTING WITH CANADIAN AMETHYST

Canadian Amethyst transports you directly to the mountain range that is its home. It lifts you above the mountains to the etheric realms where Michael and his consort, Faith, reside and lets you call on them whenever you need guidance. Working with Canadian Amethyst also facilitates spontaneous soul purification and a release of emotional baggage you may have carried through many lifetimes, so you are ready to receive a transfusion of spiritual light.

Making an Archangel Connection

Working with Canadian Amethyst or one of the other archangel crystals enables you to find healing, peace, and wisdom. Whenever you need additional protection or guidance, hold your stone and ask it to connect you to the appropriate archangel.

PREPARATION

The only preparation necessary is to keep your crystal purified in case you need it urgently and to respectfully request permission to connect to this site.

THE CONNECTION

Before you fall asleep at night, hold your archangel crystal to your forehead. Ask that it connect you to Michael and Faith or to any archangel you choose. Then place the crystal under your pillow. As you close your eyes, ask that the archangels make their presence known. If you have a petition or a question, place this before them so that it can be answered while you sleep. Then ask for your soul to be transported to the archangelic retreat to receive healing and inspiration as you sleep. Feel your soul being lifted up in a great flame of light, love, and protection.

In the morning, thank the archangels and the crystal. Keep your crystal with you to anchor the contact.

The tranquillity of Lake Louise encourages spiritual connection. ▶

Tyb's Story: Touched by an Angel

My experience at Lake Louise was very profound. I did not immediately know I was visited by Archangel Michael. But an Angelic "Light Being" touched me. I [had] found an enchanted brook-side faerie den, resplendent in bright lime-green moss and iridescent yellow lichen. It was dotted with two striking striated lavender boulders. Amazing sandstone . . . purple quartz. Amethyst! It was and remains an enchanted and beautiful power spot.

A visible beam of light and connected on my chest. I thought it was one of the angled sunbeams, then the energy jolted me and I saw kaleidoscopic colors everywhere and felt the presence of an Angelic Being. I actually saw a formless, yet intense massive golden light over half the length of the lake. The energy connected to my heart center, in an elongated beam. A blue sphere, glowing golden-yellow in its inner core, formed a few feet from where I sat. I felt a tremendous divinity. I had one of the most powerful internal reviews of my life. I was able to pray deeply on each aspect of my life, goals, and spiritual purpose. I connected deeply to the Angelic Energy and understood the anchoring to the lake.

Alternative Crystals

The Rocky Mountains are filled with minerals, metals, and crystal treasures. Red Quartz, Gold in Quartz, Jasper, and Ammolite connect to Lake Louise. The crystals listed for other archangel retreats connect to those archangels.

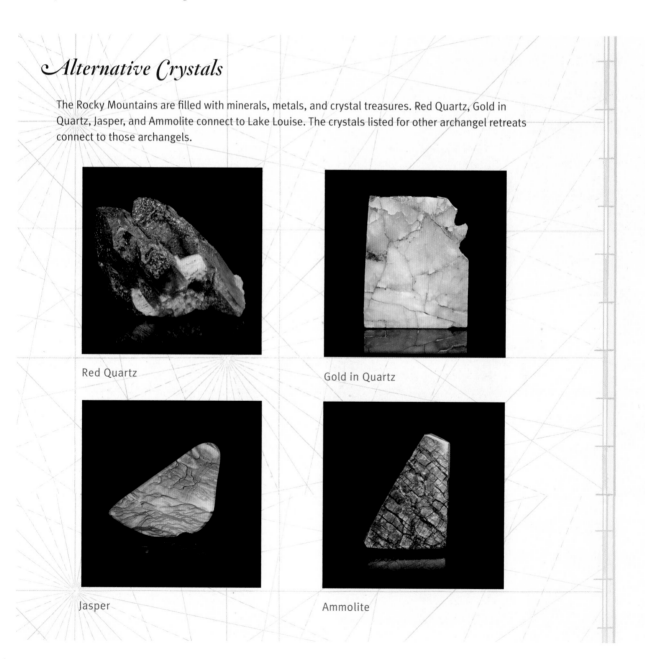

Red Quartz

Gold in Quartz

Jasper

Ammolite

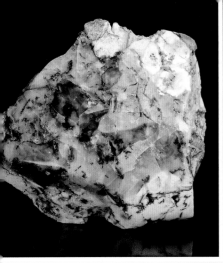

Chapter 7

THE
COSMIC PORTAL

— MOUNT SHASTA, CASCADE RANGE —

"Lonely as God, and white as a winter moon, Mount Shasta starts up sudden and solitary from the heart of the great black forests of Northern California."

—Joaquin Miller, Life Amongst the Modocs

SACRED SITE
MOUNT SHASTA, CASCADE
RANGE, SISKIYOU COUNTY,
NORTHERN CALIFORNIA 41°18'
N 122°18' W

CORRESPONDING CRYSTAL
MOUNT SHASTA BLUE OPAL

The second highest volcano in the United States, Mount Shasta is one of seven major energy centers of the world. Visiting this mountain has been described as a pilgrimage to a great outdoor cathedral. Mount Shasta Opal, a blue stone found near the mountain, activates the power vortex and draws in higher dimensions.

✳ Mount Shasta, Cascade Range, Northern California

What this site offers you

- Access to your power
- A portal to ascension
- Facilitation of the descent of high-vibration energies to Earth
- Ability to deepen your respect for the Earth as a living being

Crystal Connections

Mount Shasta is an active volcano, although currently quiescent. In volcanic landscapes, a continual creation process goes on. Molten magma is thrust up from the bowels of the Earth to create new land and is then eroded down again, so the mountain constantly changes form. Basalt, the main volcanic plug, is a hard plutonic rock that assists you in exploring your inner self. Encouraging emotional detachment, it imparts strength of mind. This rock instills stability and support during times of change or trauma and helps you bounce back from life's challenges, encouraging personal growth.

Some crystals found around the mountain, such as Opal, have undergone immense change. Working with the crystals associated with this site helps you recognize the long cycle of transmutation that occurs on Earth and how one thing morphs into another.

Quartz is an important part of the energetic construction of the mountain; indigenous people called Quartz "the brains of Mother Earth." Serpentine, a deeply shamanic, shapeshifting stone that grounds spiritual endeavors, is also found here. It helps you feel more in control of your life. Gold was discovered in this region in the 1850s and led to the displacement of the local tribes from their ancient lands. A story from the early 1900s describes the interior of the mountain:

> *"The walls, polished as by jewelers, though excavated by Giants, floors carpeted with long, fleecy gray fabric that looked like fur, but was a mineral product; ledges intersected by the builders and in their wonderful polish exhibiting veinings of gold, of silver, of green copper ores, and maculations of precious stones."*
>
> —*Phylos the Tibetan (Frederick Spencer Oliver),*
> A Dweller on Two Planets

Snowcapped Mount Shasta with its forest skirts and reflective lake. ▶

Mount Shasta: The center of creation.

The Cosmic Portal: Mount Shasta

Visible for many miles in every direction, snowcapped Mount Shasta has skirts of green with hot and cold springs streaming from its base. Unique weather patterns and strange lenticular cloud formations lend it an aura of supernatural power, and it is regarded as a fountain of cosmic energy. Designated the retreat of Archangel Gabriel and home of the ascended master Saint Germain, it represents Taurus on the world landscape zodiac. Mount Shasta has constant low-level geothermal activity and a complex structure. Native people believe it is inhabited by a powerful Earth energy spirit. Reports of strange lights, fireballs, eerie sounds, and UFO landings have given the mountain a reputation as an intergalactic cosmic portal, a "stargate" that attracts beings from outer space. New Agers and ascension-

seekers travel here to access the power, meditate, communicate with the spirit world, and be healed. Since the 1880s, it has been associated with the lost land of Lemuria, and an ancient Lemurian race is rumored to inhabit caves in the mountain. Many people believe that a huge golden crystal exists in the fifth dimension above this site, creating a temple that can be accessed in meditation or by shamanic journeying.

MOUNT SHASTA'S SACRED TRADITIONS

Mount Shasta was sacred to many native tribes and stood at the meeting place of four nation territories. Artifacts suggest a continuous presence at the site for more than 9,000 years. Native peoples revered Mount Shasta as a place of healing, but they kept their ceremonies and habitation below the treeline as the mountain was deemed too powerful to live on. Traditionally, medicine men and women were brought here for shamanic training, to learn the arts of healing and soul retrieval and the properties of therapeutic plants. It was said that Mount Shasta is the beginning and the end of all life, a place from which you ascended into the sky along the Milky Way into All That Is. Because the mountain represented the paternal grandparents of the Pit River Tribe, it was known as "Grandfather."

Today, the Wintu Tribe lives around Mount Shasta where they conduct ceremonies, rituals, and sweat lodges. They orientate their dead toward the mountain so that their souls fly to the top and from there up to the Milky Way. Tradition says Chief Skell ascended to the heavens from the mountain's summit.

SACRED ACOUSTICS

Sound is important to the indigenous people of Shasta. They reportedly found many tunnels inside the mountain that produce a sound that can be interpreted to provide guidance. According to the Wintus, another realm exists within the mountain, accessed via vents or caves. Such places are guarded by spirits, or mountain boys, who sometimes speak to local shamans.

CHAKRA CONNECTION

Mount Shasta is considered the root, or base, chakra that underpins our collective survival. As long as this chakra is fully functioning, all will be well with the human race; but if the site is disrupted—by an eruption, for example—humanity's survival is in peril. A prophecy from the time when the native tribes were displaced says that if Mount Shasta loses its snow and glaciers, its next eruption is drawing close.

MYTHOLOGY, LEGENDS, AND LORE

One legend says Mount Shasta was created when the Chief of the Sky Spirits grew tired of his home in the cold "Above," so he poured earth, rock, and snow through a hole in the sky into the darkness below. He used this mound to step down into the world and added plants, animals, and trees to a landscape watched over by grizzly bears. Bestowing the mountain with spiritual significance, he added the Sun to light the world. Pleased with his handiwork, he hollowed out the center of the mound and took up residence. The smoke that billowed from the top of the crater came from his chimney. However, his daughter fell from the mountain and married a grizzly bear. Their children were the first humans. Angered, the god condemned the bears to walk on four legs.

The story is a profound metaphor for the presence of the divine in creation. According to local tribes, various animals had a hand in creating Mount Shasta. One said that Owl sought fire here, another that Mole began the mountain, and yet another that the animals fashioned Obsidian arrowheads to shoot at human beings. According to another Indian myth, a powerful spirit called Mis Misa lives inside the mountain and keeps the universe in balance.

THE LEMURIAN LINK

During the mid-1800s, a legend circulated that Lemurian exiles from the lost continent lived in the mountain. In 1931, the Rosicrucians published a book declaring this to be a corner of the lost land of Lemuria, an advanced civilization lost millennia ago to a flood. In 1939, Edgar Larkin, an amateur astronomer, told the *Los Angeles Star* that he had observed these people with his telescope. He described very tall beings with short-cropped white hair.

The story quickly took hold and believers claimed these beings were about 14,000 years old, predating Atlantis. They reputedly still patronize a store in Weed, California, paying for their supplies with gold nuggets. Another race inhabiting the mountain, the Yaktayvians, supposedly live in gold-encrusted caves and clang magical bells to keep away the curious. By the mid-1960s, tales were being told of the Great White Brotherhood, UFO landings, meetings with alien beings, and occasional sightings of the elusive Bigfoot.

Mount Shasta Blue Opal

The Portal Activator: Mount Shasta Blue Opal

One of the few stones actually found at its corresponding sacred site, Mount Shasta Blue Opal connects you to this immense energy portal. This high-vibration stone activates the cosmic portal and powerful energy vortex held by Mount Shasta. Opal is traditionally a stone of protection, faithfulness, and loyalty that induces mystical visions and psychic journeying. It conveys invisibility upon you when you need to travel clandestinely.

MOUNT SHASTA OPAL'S PROPERTIES

A calming stone that quiets the mind and eases sleep problems, Opal is tranquil and nurturing. Mount Shasta Opal also calms fears. If you fear cataclysmic changes or global warming, Mount Shasta Opal reassures you that all will be well. It helps assimilate energetic changes within your physical body, so that the ascension process happens here on Earth as all beings become part of unity consciousness. If you experienced similar evolutionary changes in previous lifetimes in the far past, Mount Shasta Opal de-energizes any residual traumatic imprint. It lets you find emotional healing and face the prospect of change with equanimity.

Mount Shasta Opal is a powerful shamanic stone that helps you travel stealthily during metaphysical workings of all kinds, especially during soul retrieval. It opens the third eye, soma, and higher crown chakras so you communicate with the ascended masters and angelic beings.

Blue Opals assist in releasing communication blockages and enable you to deal more calmly with stress. They help you connect to your spiritual purpose. All Opals reflect the energies of the wearer and ensure that your intentions are for the highest good of all when working with this stone. Use it to radiate peace, love, and higher vibrations into the environment around you.

SAINT GERMAIN

Mount Shasta has become home to many New Age movements. In 1930, G. W. Ballard climbed the mountain to commune with nature. While bending over a stream, he felt an electric tingle run through his body. Turning, he saw a young man standing before him who said that if Ballard gave him the cup he would give him a much more refreshing drink. When Ballard drank, he gasped with surprise at the marvelous taste and tonic effect. The young man explained that it came straight from the Universal Supply and introduced himself as the legendary Saint Germain. Ballard described him as "a magnificent Godlike figure—in a white jeweled robe, a Light and Love sparkling in his eyes." Ballard established the I AM, or Saint Germain, Foundation at the foot of the mountain, where it remains.

MOUNT SHASTA OPAL'S HEALING POWER

Mount Shasta Opal is an excellent tonic for the throat and eyes. Opal traditionally assists blood sugar swings. The stone heals the etheric and karmic blueprints from which your physical body arose.

CONNECTING WITH MOUNT SHASTA OPAL

Hold Mount Shasta Opal to your third eye to open your metaphysical abilities and connect you to All That Is.

Mount Shasta Meditation

This meditation opens your own cosmic portal and connects you to the power of Mount Shasta. It takes you far above our planet to look down on your Earthly home.

PREPARATION

Cleanse and dedicate your stone to your highest good before commencing the meditation. Choose a time and place where you will not be disturbed. Respectfully request permission to connect to this site.

THE MEDITATION

Hold your Opal to your third eye. Feel it carrying you to the top of the mountain. From there, you can journey to the Milky Way and beyond to gain cosmic wisdom, or stay on the summit to meet the ascended masters.

When it's time to return, look down at the Earth. See our beautiful blue planet hanging in space. Allow your heart to open to your home and feel the need to care deeply for it.

When you've finished the meditation, put your Opal down. Consciously close the portal by imagining shutters closing over it.

Alternative Crystals

Serpentine and Quartz are found in the vicinity of Mount Shasta. Consciousness-raising, man-made Lavender Ruby Quartz is available from an outlet near the mountain. To access the fifth-dimensional temple, use Golden Quartz, such as Golden Healer or Rainbow Mayanite, that has extremely high vibrations.

Ruby Lavender Quartz

Rainbow Mayanite

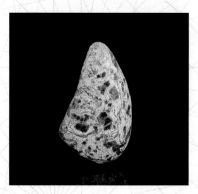

Serpentine

Chapter 8

VORTICES OF AWESOME BEAUTY

— SEDONA, ARIZONA —

"During my time in Sedona I have discovered that a vortex isn't about a certain place which gives you a predetermined feeling. For me the word vortex is more like a concept where we can begin to explore our relationship to ourselves and the world around us. Our busy lives have taken the focus off us and our connection to the land. The power of a place like Sedona—the power of a vortex— can help to restore us to a more balanced state of being."

—www.innerjourneys.us

SACRED SITE
SEDONA, ARIZONA, UNITED
STATES 34°51' N 111°47' W

CORRESPONDING CRYSTAL
SEDONA STONE

Magnificent crimson peaks tower above deep red canyons at this site, which has been sacred for millennia. According to Indian legend, this is where humans come face to face with their true nature. The Sedona region has more energy vortices than any other site on Earth. Stones from this region retain Sedona's vibrant energy, no matter how far they travel.

Crystal Connections

The ancient rock of Sedona is an iron-rich Sandstone that weathers into fantastic shapes and amazing colors that look like a layer cake. It is studded with white (Snow) Quartz. Small pieces of the rock break off into pebbles and, with permission, they can be used to connect to the site. The area was once covered by ocean, and fossils and seashells are found in the Sandstone's gray-white bands. Around the village of Oak Creek Basalt deposits attest to the landscape's volcanic nature.

Sedona Power

For thousands of years, American Indians have performed sacred ceremonies at Sedona. Although the whole landscape is awesomely beautiful, the energy vortices are what draw people from around the world. A vortex is where you most strongly plug into the multidimensional Sedona spiritual energy. The main vortices occur at four locations—Bell Rock, Airport Mesa, Cathedral Rock, and Boynton Canyon—but minor vortices and additional, highly energetic places also occur.

> *"There exists an open door to possibilities in life much larger than the limits of our minds. What we may call a vortex the Native Americans may call sacred ground."*
>
> *www.innerjourneys.us*

Earth energy lines, or telluric currents, follow the circulation of magnetic and electrical flows within the Earth. The energies are cyclical and seasonal, fluctuating and self-renewing. Where two or more Earth energy meridians cross, a powerful psychic vortex results. The ancients recognized these power spots, which concentrate natural healing energies and shamanic power, and sited sacred places accordingly.

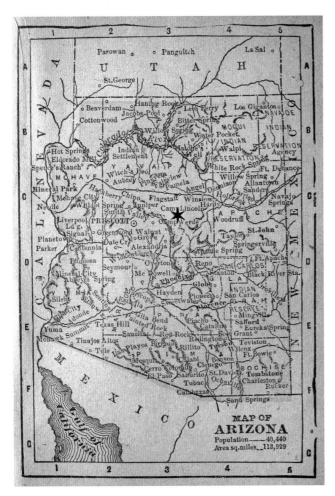

✳ Sedona, Arizona

What this site offers you

- Connection to the awesome power of the Earth
- Psychic and spiritual expansion
- Past-life awareness

Tapping the potential of nature.

Indian legend says the Great Spirit gives birth to rainbows at Sedona's vortices. Vortices may be electric, magnetic, or a combination: electromagnetic. Vortices are acupuncture points on the Earth's energy meridians. Positive, or yang, vortices generate energy, charging the body and the Earth; negative, or yin, ones dissipate energy and open psychic abilities. Bell Rock and Airport Mesa at Sedona are electric vortices; Courthouse Butte and Cathedral Rock are magnetic; Boynton Canyon is electromagnetic. Although everyone perceives the energy differently, magnetic vortices tend to be yin, and electric or electromagnetic ones to be yang. Common responses include an enhanced feeling of well-being, expanded spiritual awareness, fresh insights, immense feelings of joy, and a sense of being wired or "flying" that lasts for days.

MYTHOLOGY, LEGENDS, AND LORE

Many New Agers believe Sedona is an ancient Lemurian site with a buried city or an enormous crystal beneath it. Local Indians have long held this land sacred. Komwida Pokwee (Old Woman Rock), a goddess with supernatural powers, lived here and gave her ancient knowledge to the local Yavapai Indians through her grandson, Skata-amcha.

According to oral mythology, there were four cycles of creation. The first humans emerged from underground and were drowned in a flood. Komwida Pokwee and her grandson were part of the second cycle. The third ended in a huge fire. We are now living in the fourth cycle. Komwida Pokwee continued to give guidance to the Yavapai medicine men until the tribe became scattered and lost. In another version, each world started in balance and harmony but was disrupted: the first world by ice, the next by fire, the third by water.

The towering sandstone pillars of Sedona radiate power.

Sedona Stone

A variation of the myth, passed down through Mike Harrison at the turn of the twentieth century, says:

> "We call that girl Kamalapukwia. That means 'Old Lady White Stone.' She had a white stone [presumably Snow Quartz]. And that white stone is the one which protects the women . . . She is the first woman and we come from her. She came out at Sedona and that's where all Indians come from . . . [her grandson was] Sakarakaamche. He gave us four sacred things: the black root, the yellow powder, the blue stone and the white stone . . . The blue stone and the white stone, that's what protects us from bad things. The blue stone stands for men, the white stone for the women. When you have these stones and think well, bad things can't hit you. The blue stone that people wear on a ring [presumably Turquoise], that's not the one that protects them. It is like a toy. But when it is blessed by a medicine man, then it will help."

Quoted in Dick Sutphen's
Sedona: Psychic Energy Vortexes

Awesome Crystallized Energy: Sedona Stone

A rich, rusty-red Sandstone colored by oxidizing iron, Sedona Stone holds the concentrated energy of the powerful multidimensional vortices and links to universal knowledge. It stimulates metaphysical sight, inner sight, and out-of-body journeying. Holding Sedona Stone plugs you into an inexhaustible source of power.

SEDONA STONE'S PROPERTIES

Sedona Stone is pure crystallized energy—even the smallest pebble contains the resonance of the energy vortices. Used during ceremonies and shamanic journeying, this stone enhances your metaphysical abilities, especially if placed over the soma chakra in the center of your hairline. The vortex whirls you deep within yourself to explore your inner dimensions.

Alternative Crystals

Arizona is rich in gemstones. Peridot, Quartz, Turquoise, Amethyst, Shattuckite, and Ajoite harness the power of the vortices.

Peridot

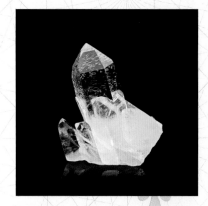

Clear Quartz

Turquoise

Amethyst

Shattuckite

Ajoite

SEDONA STONE'S HEALING POWER

Sedona Stone is an immensely powerful healing stone with rejuvenating and revitalizing properties. The energy imbued into the stone passes into the physical and subtle bodies as a heightened sense of physical and spiritual well-being. It reenergizes all the cells of the body, as well as the blood and lymph.

CONNECTING WITH SEDONA STONE

This stone plugs you into a gigantic power source. Holding it immediately transports you into the Earth's energetic grid and power-generating vortex points.

The Sedona Experience

This meditation allows you to experience Sedona's energies in whatever way is appropriate for you. The experience is heightened by a Google Earth virtual tour of the site to select a vortex connection point.

PREPARATION

Ensure that you will not be disturbed. If the stone has come straight from Sedona without much handling by other people, it may not need cleansing. Respectfully request permission to connect to this site.

THE EXPERIENCE

Sit quietly, holding your stone. Allow the energy to flow up your arms and into whatever part of your body is appropriate. Feel yourself being plugged into an energy vortex in Sedona. Relax and enjoy your own unique experience of this awesome place.

When you have finished, put the stone down and consciously disconnect. Feel your connection to your body and the Earth beneath your feet.

David's Experience: Sacred Stones of Sedona

As the plane approached the mountains near Sedona, I felt a very strong sense of being welcomed. While giving a Petaltone presentation, we were blessed to be joined by Standing Deer from the Taos Pueblo in New Mexico. The next day we were led to a secret location in the red rocks where an ancient "Grandmother Cave" became the setting for a ritual offering with Standing Deer. Below the cave was an old medicine wheel made of the local rocks. Standing Deer commenced his drum chant. I've always loved sacred caves; being enclosed by the rock enables a deep communion with the Earth. The native ceremonies are often so simple, but leave one feeling touched by the sacredness of earth, rock, and plants as well as animals. The red rocks of Sedona are alive with the ancestral heritage of the landscape, and the ancestors are tangibly present. I find that these beings wish to communicate, and seem to be very happy that people are interested in the energies of the landscape and the expanding of consciousness. There's a real no-nonsense feel about the energies of these rocks, and I realize that the native peoples of all lands have that connection to work with.

Chapter 9

THE PLACE OF PEACE

— PIPESTONE NATIONAL MONUMENT —

"When you pray with this pipe, you pray for and with everything."
—Black Elk, Oglala Lakota medicine man

SACRED SITE
PIPESTONE NATIONAL MONU-
MENT, MINNESOTA, UNITED
STATES 44°0' N 96°19' W

CORRESPONDING CRYSTAL
PIPESTONE (CATLINITE)

Pipestone National Monument was the first national monument created in the United States, in the 1930s. However, the site's history spans millennia, and it was of enormous spiritual importance to American Indian cultures. Oral tradition tells us that all who entered Pipestone put aside their weapons. The Great Spirit had declared the site sacrosanct. Warring tribes quarried peacefully side by side for the soft red clay they shaped into pipe bowls and ritual objects used in ceremonies. The oldest pipes date back to 1500 BCE. Pipestone smoke carries messages to the Great Spirit.

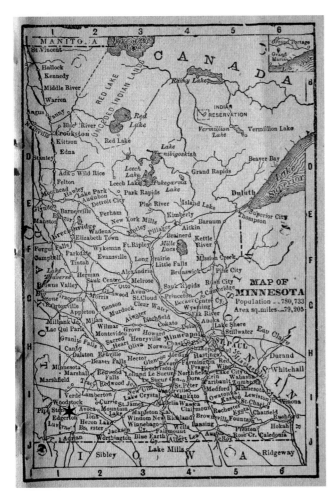

* Pipestone, Minnesota

Crystal Connections

Pipestone is more than 1.6 billion years old. A combination of Diaspore, Pyrophyllite, Muscovite, and Hematite—all of which have potent healing and metaphysical properties. Pipestone was traded across the United States from Georgia to the Pacific Coast.

One of the few stones quarried in situ at a sacred site, the Catlinite band of red clay sits beneath a hard layer of Quartzite that must be carefully removed. Quartzite, one of the hardest known crystals, imparts a powerful energetic resonance to the underlying clay. The clay deposit lies beneath a layer of glacial drift with Basalt and Quartzite, a metamorphosed Sandstone. Sandstone is a fluid stone with an abundance of Qi; Quartzite is highly energetic as is Basalt, a strongly magnetic rock that keeps the Earth's meridians in balance. These rocks, moved by glaciers from hundreds of miles away, would have stood out on the stoneless prairie—no wonder people approached the site with awe.

At the quarry's entrance lie huge erratics—boulders transported by ice for hundreds of miles and which are of a geology alien to the landscape where they were finally deposited. These boulders contain sparkling Feldspar and Mica, and are revered as guardian beings. All around the quarry, weathered Quartzite and Pipestone rocks display simulacra: human faces in the stone. But it is the Pipestone that connects you directly to the peace of the site.

At the entrance to the Pipestone monument, alongside Lake Hiawatha, sit the "Three Maidens." These are guardian stones, huge glacial erratic boulders. At one time, seventy ancient petroglyphs on thirty-five slabs of rock surrounded the stones. Some have been removed to the museum to prevent vandalism; others are scattered elsewhere. At the Three Maidens, tribes seeking permission from the spirits to quarry at the site make offerings of tobacco. From the Maidens the path winds alongside the creek to the quarry face, passing various other guardian stones en route.

What this site offers you

- Immense sense of peace and calm
- Respect for the Earth as a sacred, living being
- Forgiveness and reconciliation
- Healing for loss of land, tribe, or home
- Reconnection to American Indian heritage
- An opportunity to honor the old ways, regardless of your cultural background
- The potential to walk lightly on sacred ground

Pipestone National Monument

This sacred site willingly offers up its stone. There is a continuing tradition of stone extraction here, but quarrying licenses are granted only to American Indians. Archaeological evidence suggests Pipestone's quarries have been used for more than 3,000 years. From around 1700, the Pipestone site, known as Iyansha K'apt, the Place Where One Digs the Red Rock, was under the guardianship of the Yankton Dakota nation. In the mid-1880s, with the establishment of the new town of Pipestone, the Dakota were moved off the land to a reservation 150 miles (241 km) away, making access to the quarry difficult. They spent decades claiming compensation for the loss of their sacred site. In 1928, they were paid $338,558.90 for the land, but they lost any claim to the quarry itself. After years of conflict between settlers and tribes, in 1937 the site was returned to the spiritual guardianship of its native owners.

An immensely quiet, wooded site with few tourists, Pipestone National Monument needs to be approached in quiet contemplation to feel its great age and sanctity. The energy shimmers in the sunlight. Sacred for millennia, the site was revered for its unique position and its red stone, which could be carved easily. George Catlin, one of the first European Americans to visit this site, describes what a paradise it was and the impact it had on those who made the pilgrimage to collect the sacred stone:

> "[We crossed] one of the most beautiful prairie countries in the world. This tract of country is mostly covered with the richest soil, and furnishes an abundance of good water, which flows from a thousand living springs. For many miles we had the Coteau [hill] in view in the distance before us, which looked like a blue cloud settling down in the horizon. When we at length reached the summit . . . there was not a tree or bush to be seen in any direction. On the very top of this mount we found the far-famed quarry or fountain of the Red Pipe, which is truly an anomaly in nature. . . .

> The principal and most striking feature of this place is a perpendicular wall of close-grained, compact quartz running nearly North–South with its face to the West. . . . [A small stream] is now left to glide for some distance over a perfectly level surface of quartz rock; and then to leap from the top of the wall into a deep basin below. . . . This beautiful wall is horizontal and stratified in several distinct layers of light gray, and rose or flesh-coloured quartz, and for most of the way, both on the front of the wall, and for acres of its horizontal surface, highly polished or glazed as if by ignition. . . .

> At the base of the wall and on the very ground where the Indians dig for the red stone, rests a group of five stupendous boulders of gneiss, leaning against each other; the smallest of which is twelve or fifteen feet high, and the largest twenty five feet in diameter. . . . The surface of these boulders is in every part covered with a grey moss, which gives them an extremely ancient and venerable appearance. . . .

> With such notes on this shorn land, whose quiet and silence are only broken by the winds and the thunders of Heaven, I close my note-book."

> From the letters of George Catlin,
> www.rocksandminerals.com

Sadly, the geologist in Catlin showed little respect for sanctity, chipping bits off the boulders and later, when they became too heavy to carry, discarding them.

LEGENDS, LORE, AND MYTHOLOGY

Each of the nations who came to Pipestone had its own stories about the origins of the pipe and Pipestone. George Catlin recounts one legend:

> "At an ancient time the Great Spirit, in the form of a large bird, stood upon the wall of rock and called all the tribes around him. Taking out a piece of the red stone, he formed it into a pipe and smoked it, the smoke rolling over the whole multitude. He then told his red children that this red stone was their flesh, that they were made from it, that they must all smoke to him through it, that they must use it for nothing but pipes; and as it belonged alike to all the tribes, the ground was sacrosanct, and no weapons must be used or brought upon it."

In another story, told by Black Elk, a bundle was presented to the people by White Buffalo Calf Woman. Before she shapeshifted into a white buffalo calf, she said

"Behold this and always love it! It is lela wakan [very sacred], and you must treat it as such. No impure man should ever be allowed to see it, for within the bundle there is a sacred pipe. With this you will, during the winters to come, send your voices to Wakan-Tanka, your Father and Grandfather. With this pipe you will walk upon the Earth, for the Earth is your Grandmother and Mother, and She is sacred. Every step that is taken upon Her should be as a prayer. The bowl of this pipe is of red stone, it is the Earth. Carved in the stone and facing the center is this buffalo calf who represents all the four-leggeds who live upon your Mother. The stem of the pipe is wood and this represents all that grows upon the Earth. And these twelve feathers which hang here where the stem fits into the bowl are from Wanbli Galeshka, the Spotted Eagle, and they represent the eagle and all the winged of the air. All these peoples and all the things of the universe are joined to you who smoke the pipe—all send their voices to Wakan-Tanka the Great Sprit."

A modern-day Lakota, Lame Deer, tells another legend. At the start of creation Wakan-Tanka, the Great Spirit, was angry with his people and allowed Unktehi, the water monster, to flood the land. The hill that today forms the Pipestone quarry remained above water, and the people quickly climbed to the top. But waves smashed over the top and all the people were killed, except one young girl. Wanbli Galeshka, a big eagle, flew her to a lone stone pinnacle in the Black Hills. From their union, the Lakota Oyate, or eagle nation, was born. The blood of the people who had been killed soaked into the land and became Pipestone. The quarry, formed from the blood of the ancestors, is therefore sacred.

CEREMONIAL MEANING

The pipes were stored in animal-skin pouches or in bundles with other sacred objects and used for ceremonial purposes. Treasured pipes were often interred with the dead.

"All the meanings of moral duty, ethics, religious, and spiritual conceptions were symbolized in the pipe. It signified brotherhood, peace, and the perfection of Wakan-Tanka, and to the Lakota the pipe stood for that which the Bible, church, state, and flat, all combined represented to the mind of the white man."

Chief Standing Bear, Ponca chief

At age nineteen, Frank Grouard was captured by the Lakota and spent seven years in the camps of Chiefs Sitting Bull and Crazy Horse. In his biography, he described the pipe ceremony:

"The pipe figures in each and every Indian ceremonial. When lit in council or during religious rites or when used at dances or feasts, it passed from left to right and never from right to left. It was usual for the chief or warrior lighting the pipe to offer some particular spirit the first draught of smoke, and the stem of the pipe was then held toward the different points of the compass, the sun, moon, stars, or any object to which the holder of the pipe desired to offer homage. This little ceremony was never omitted. Before passing the pipe, . . . each Indian inhaled as much smoke as his lung cavity permitted, and the smoke was afterward expelled at his pleasure. They used different pipes at the different ceremonials and would scorn to sanction the use of the council pipe in any other place or on any other occasion."

The poet Henry Wadsworth Longfellow in his epic *Song of Hiawatha* sets out another use for the Pipestone site. It was a sacred gathering place for five warring tribes to come together in peace:

"On the Mountains of the Prairie,
On the great Red Pipe-stone Quarry,
Gitche Manito, the mighty,
He the Master of Life, descending,
On the red crags of the quarry
Stood erect, and called the nations,
Called the tribes of men together."

Pipestone quarry, on the *Coteau des Prairies*, George Catlin, 1836–37

COSMOLOGICAL ORIENTATION

The Pipestone ridge runs almost due north–south, and the quarry faces west. An important equinoctial marker for the changing seasons, the moon rises and sets almost due east–west at the spring and autumn equinoxes—a fact that the nations would have noted, given the importance of the four directions to their ceremonies.

QUARRYING

Quarrying Pipestone is a laborious process, taking between two and six weeks. It is carried out by hand with due deference. Describing his visit to the quarry in 1836, George Catlin reported the care with which the stone was mined. The guardian boulders, which ice lodged on top of the ridge, were particularly sacred:

"[the] veneration of them is such that not a spear of grass is broken or bent by his feet, within three or four rods of them, where he stops, and in humble supplication, by throwing plugs of tobacco to them, solicits permission to dig and carry away the red stone for his pipes."

The fragile 2- to 12-inch (5 to 30 cm) layered bands of Pipestone clay lie under a topping of pink Quartzite, which currently is between 4 and 17 feet (1.2 and 5.2 m) thick. This exceedingly hard upper layer is taken out with sledgehammers and wedges. All the topsoil and Quartzite is wheelbarrowed away from the site and placed into carefully constructed walls to prevent collapse. Initially, Pipestone was close to the surface and its discovery was linked to the buffalo, a sacred animal, as Joseph Nicollet recorded in 1838:

> "The discovery of the red earth is due to the passage of buffalo which hollowed out a deep pathway as they do in the regions of seasonal migration where they try always to take the same route. The pathway revealed the surface of the red rock. One can imagine, then, in nations for whom the pipe is among the most important of necessary objects what a windfall it was to be provided with a soft stone of their favorite color, suitable for making pipes, in an immense land where there is no other workable rock. The pathway made formerly by the passage of animals is still clearly visible for nearly a mile, and one can see that the Indians mined the red stone there for many years before being forced to remove rock that covered the red stone where it is now worked."

Connecting with Great Spirit: Pipestone (Catlinite)

Pipestone (Catlinite)

Pipestone has been sacred for thousands of years and must be treated with reverence and respect. Found only in one place, the southwest corner of Minnesota, Pipestone unites the spiritual and physical worlds and invokes a profound connection to the Great Spirit. Fortunately, you can energetically connect with the stone by looking at a photograph.

PIPESTONE'S PROPERTIES

A soft, red clay with white flecks, Pipestone helps honor the old ways and the ceremonies that upheld them, teaching that everything is divine and joined. We are part of nature and nature is an inseparable part of us, just as we are an integral part of universal consciousness. Pipestone unites the spiritual and physical worlds, sending prayers to the Great Spirit, and yet grounding them in the everyday world. This stone brings everything into the present moment, the eternal now. It helps you walk lightly upon the Earth, honoring its sacredness and that of everything upon it.

Meditating with Pipestone creates a calm inner center, where nothing disturbs your serenity. It lets you radiate peace into your environment. Use the stone to explore the American Indian culture or to connect to your own ancestral line, especially if that included ethnic conflict or dispossession. Grid Pipestone around an area, or on a map, to bring peace to areas of environmental damage or disharmony, where animals have been slaughtered without thought, or where there is deep sadness in and for the land. The stone has been used in ceremonies to honor the dispossessed—those who have lost their homes and land—to bring peace to their souls. It also brings peace to those who, in other lives, have lost their land or families.

Pipestone is an excellent crystal for past-life healing. It replaces guilt, shame, or anger with forgiveness, reconciliation, and peace. Placed over the Earth star chakra beneath the feet, it deenergizes negative feelings and transmutes them, sending unconditional love into Mother Earth and to the incarnated soul.

PIPESTONE'S HEALING POWER

For eons, Pipestone has been revered as a healing stone. Its greatest gift is inner peace and core stability. Reportedly carvers of genuine Pipestone never suffer from dust inhalation, even if they have asthma. Therefore, it is regarded among American Indians as a lung healer as well as a master crystal.

CONNECTING WITH PIPESTONE

Harnessing the power of Pipestone instills a deep, unshakable inner peace and connects you to All That Is. (Always ask permission first.) Hold it to attune to its healing resonance and the unity consciousness at its heart. Meditating with Pipestone connects you to guides from the native tradition, invoking healing and essential teachings. Placed in the center of a medicine wheel, it is an excellent adjunct to a ceremony. Performing the following Pipestone ceremony reconnects you with the wisdom of ancient ancestors and the Earth's healing power.

Alternative Crystal

Catlinite from locations near Pipestone is often sold as Pipestone, but it tends to fragment into dust rather than being easy to carve. It can be used in ceremonies if the spirit of Pipestone is first invited in, as can Catlinite or Steatite from other locations.

Steatite

The Oracle, simulcra in stone.

The Pipestone Ceremony

This ceremony connects you to All That Is and helps heal pain caused by the loss of land or family. Even if you don't have a piece of actual Pipestone and have only seen a picture, Pipestone calls you to its sacred home—especially if you have healing work to do on your past or are being asked to heal on behalf of the collective.

PREPARATION

Respectfully request permission to visit this site. Purify your stone in the smoke of a smudge stick, and then purify the four directions by blowing smoke to them. Face each direction in turn and call in the spirits of the south, west, north, and east, and then above and below, asking them to sanctify your sacred space. Settle yourself in the middle of the space facing toward Minnesota. Consider making an offering of tobacco or light a pipe if this feels appropriate. If you do not have a piece of Pipestone, simply gaze at the photograph in this book and ask that it attune you to its vibration. You could watch the slide show on the Pipestone National Monument website (www.nps.gov/pipe) when asking the Oracle to guide your journey, as it effectively conveys you into a sense of place. An American Indian drumming or chanting CD deepens this experience.

CEREMONY

Hold your Catlinite or place it on the floor in front of you if it is too large to hold. Ask permission to enter this sacred site. Focus on the illustration of the Pipestone Oracle (opposite). Ask the Oracle to guide your journey.

In your mind's eye, make your way along the ancient track to the cliff face. Sit cross-legged on the ground. Tune into this ancient place. Feel the pain of all who have lost their land and their nationhood, no matter where in the world they may be. Shed healing tears for them. If you have lost your own land or home, honor your feelings and your loss. Give them voice.

Feel the peace of Pipestone suffusing your being, transmuting the pain and longing into a sense of belonging. Feel it connect you to All That Is. Let this feeling flow out to every corner of the Earth, taking with it forgiveness and reconnection to all the sacred land for all the beings who live in, on, or above our planet to the Great Spirit, and All That Is.

When you are ready to return, place that feeling in your heart. Bring your awareness back into the everyday world. Feel your deep connection to the Earth beneath your feet.

Chrissy's Experience: Connecting to All That Is

When I looked at the slide show on the Pipestone National Park website . . . I could sense a procession of people walking that path chanting, heads hung low. I read the quotation by Black Elk and all I could think was, this is of its time now. This quote for me reflects everything that exists around and in us and how it is all becoming apparent to us now. I've recently started talking to trees on a newer level and now when I say "I see you in me," I get this lovely whoosh of energy right through my heart. This stone is clearly a link to All That Is.

My experience developed over the days that followed. I went back to the photo and got a feeling that I'd done something bad, or witnessed something bad with this stone and the word I got was "intrusion." I knew that some serious clearing was needed. I started to cry and got the word "help." I connected with a slab of Pipestone and I felt it absorb my sorrow and dispatch it for transmuting and the tears evaporated straight away. I then called in Two Horns (my guide) and asked him to bring me an etheric Pipestone pipe that would work for my highest evolution. A little pipe came into my aura and went straight to the throat chakra. This will strengthen my voice and in turn allow me to help and heal others through my own evolution.

Chapter 10

STANDING TOGETHER

— 9/11 MEMORIAL AND HIROSHIMA —

"It's about making meaning not just for the people who know the individuals, but for the people who are going there. In that way, people can learn the human relationships and stories underneath the names themselves."

—Jake Barton, founder of Local Projects media design firm

SACRED SITES

9/11 MEMORIAL, NEW YORK CITY, NEW YORK, UNITED STATES 40°42' N 74°0' W AND HIROSHIMA PEACE MEMORIAL, JAPAN 34°39' N 132°45' E

CORRESPONDING CRYSTAL

HERKIMER DIAMOND

*F*ootprint fountains at the Twin Towers Plaza memorialize the lives lost on 9/11 when two jets were flown into the towers of the World Trade Center. Designed by architect Michael Arad, the official memorial at Ground Zero opened on September 11, 2011, to commemorate the tenth anniversary of a terrible morning. Ten years earlier, almost 3,000 people lost their lives at the World Trade Center. Enormous fear was generated, but it also turned many people inward to reexamine their larger-life priorities. The memorial's designers intended that courage and the power of friendship be celebrated rather than concentrating on the negative aspects.

Crystal Connections

Even under a city such as New York, crystals are found. In 1885, a Garnet weighing more than 10 pounds (4.5 kg) and measuring 6 inches (15.2 cm) was revealed during excavations on West 35th Street, close to Macy's department store. Herkimer Diamonds are local stones, named after Herkimer County, New York, but similar high-resonance crystals are found elsewhere. Herkimer Diamond helps you come to terms with loss and grief and to restore healing light to a place of darkness.

Twin Towers Plaza

Two of the largest fountains in the world sit on the footprint of the Twin Towers; water falls into a basin 30 feet (9.1 m) below. Around the rim of the fountain runs a bronze plaque inscribed with the names of those who died in New York City, at the Pentagon, on Flight 93 in Pennsylvania, and also at the 1993 bombing of the World Trade Center. It is intended that the fountains will run eternally in remembrance.

The names are grouped according to friendship and "adjacency requests" so that coworkers are memorialized together. Two brothers, firefighter John T. Vigiano II and police officer Joseph Vincent Vigiano, both died on 9/11. On the memorial, John's name appears at the end of his unit. Next to it, Joseph's name begins a list of the men in his unit. The two brothers' names are forever linked. Some of the connections are particularly poignant. All the members of one family are placed together, despite their mismatched surnames, including the tragedy's youngest victim, two-and-a-half-year-old Christine Hanson.

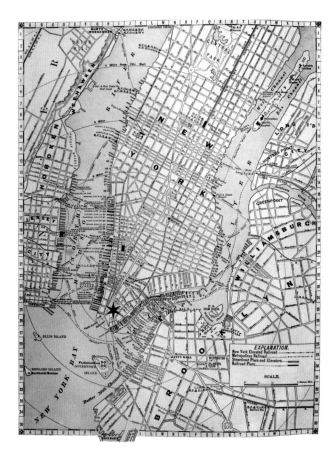

✳ Twin Towers, New York City, New York

What these sites offer you

- Coming to terms with the unbearable
- Help with mourning and moving on from loss
- Honors those who have passed on
- The power of friendship and courage
- Forgiveness and peace
- Reexamination of larger life priorities

Peace Memorial Park, Hiroshima

Stories of Heroism

"It's the connections in our lives that matter the most. These names, inscribed in bronze, are the heart of the experience."

Joe Daniels, president of 9/11 Memorial

Many stories of heroism emerged from that day. This is just one of them.

Victor Wald worked on the eighty-fourth floor of the Twin Towers. As a child, he had suffered from rheumatic fever and, racing down the stairs, he collapsed on the fifty-third floor. Many people passed him by, but Harry Ramos stopped. They had never met before, but Ramos promised not to leave him. He helped Wald down to the thirty-sixth floor but, as they got there, the building collapsed. Their names are inscribed side by side on the memorial.

◀ Two identical footprint fountains, one for each fallen tower, have been constructed and are called "Reflecting Absence."

Sister Site: Peace Memorial Park, Hiroshima

The Peace Memorial was one of the first monuments built at Hiroshima in 1952. The concrete, saddle-shaped monument covers a cenotaph holding the names of all of the people killed by the first atomic bomb. Built in Shinto style, its arched shape represents a shelter for the souls of the victims. The cenotaph carries the epitaph, "Rest in Peace, for the error shall not be repeated." Through the monument, you see the Peace Flame and the A-Bomb Dome. The flame has burned continuously since it was lit in 1964, and will remain lit until all nuclear bombs are destroyed and the planet is free from the threat of nuclear annihilation.

The Peace and Reconciliation meditation in this section is equally appropriate for either site—or anywhere atrocities have caused a mass loss of life.

Herkimer Diamond

Attuning to All That Is: Herkimer Diamond

Found in Herkimer County, New York, Herkimer Diamonds crystallize as double terminations breaking old patterns. This sparky stone stimulates creativity and conscious attunement to the highest spiritual levels, and helps you begin again after trauma or setback.

HERKIMER DIAMOND'S PROPERTIES

Despite its name and exceptional brilliance, Herkimer Diamond is Quartz. Inclusions add to its magical properties. One of the oldest Quartzes, it slowly formed underwater hundreds of millions of years ago and holds the wisdom of the ages in its crystalline depths. It attunes you to a higher reality and accelerates your spiritual growth. With an exceptionally high vibration that aligns the incarnated portion of your soul with that existing in other dimensions, Herkimer creates a powerful shield for the soul when journeying. The stone works especially well as a multidimensional information highway. Herkimer Diamond is a powerful stone of transmutation and purification; it protects against geomagnetic pollution and unblocks the chakras. Gridded around an area of environmental disharmony, it restores equilibrium.

Herkimers reprogram ingrained patterns and assist in retrieving and reintegrating parts of the soul that have fragmented in other lives. This is an excellent crystal for clearing unconscious fears and the thought forms attached to them. It helps you begin again.

HERKIMER DIAMOND'S HEALING POWER

Herkimer Diamond is a powerful detoxifying crystal that protects against electromagnetic smog and reverses its effects. By drawing energy into the body to create new neural pathways, and facilitating cellular information downloads, the crystal restructures DNA and reattunes the metabolism to a higher frequency. It helps to energetically rebuild the cellular structure in the body and heals metabolic imbalances. Herkimers create new neural pathways within the physical body that connect to the lightbody and to All That Is, so you manifest your spiritual potential here on Earth. To treat insomnia caused by environmental factors, grid Herkimer Diamonds around the bed, and cleanse the stones regularly. Herkimers energize water into a potent healing essence.

CONNECTING WITH HERKIMER DIAMOND

Connecting with this crystal breaks the past's hold on you. Herkimers act as an integrated information field that can be read to access new information, especially about your future potential.

The Peace and Reconciliation Meditation

"The World Trade Center is a living symbol of man's dedication to world peace . . . the World Trade Center should, because of its importance, become a representation of man's belief in humanity, his need for individual dignity, his beliefs in the cooperation of men, and through cooperation, his ability to find greatness."

Minoru Yamasaki, architect of the original World Trade Center

This meditation honors Yamasaki's original intention; it incorporates commemoration of the dead and comradeship in the face of adversity. Through this meditation, you send crystal light to the new buildings, the memorial garden, and the people who suffer because of the events here or similar events elsewhere.

PREPARATION

Ensure that you will not be disturbed for fifteen minutes. Respectfully request permission to connect to this site.

THE MEDITATION

Hold your Herkimer lightly in your hands. Close your eyes and breathe gently. Feel the energy of the crystal growing and glowing. A beam of light shoots out from the crystal to envelop you. Absorb this light, feeling the connection to All That Is, the deep love enfolded within it. Take that love into your heart and any painful places where loss resides. Feel the light healing and bringing peace and forgiveness to the core of your being.

Now send that light to the Twin Towers (or any other site), asking that it bring healing to all who have experienced loss. Remember those who died and the heroism shown here. Ask that peace be imbued into the memorial, and that the spirit of forgiveness and reconciliation flows into and around this place.

When you have finished, put your crystal where it continues to radiate peace and love into the world. Feel your feet making a powerful connection to the Earth. As you go about your everyday life, carry peace and healing with you.

Alternative Crystals

Substitute Arkansas, Himalayan, or other "diamonds" for Herkimer. Also consider Garnet or Agate, grounding and strengthening crystals.

Arkansas Diamond

Agate

Garnet

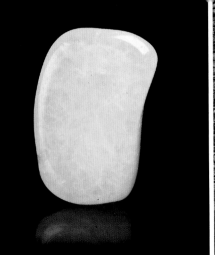

A MEGALITHIC PORTAL

— NEWGRANGE, BOYNE VALLEY, IRELAND —

"That glorious dome that stands
By the dark rolling waves of the Boyne
Where Oengus Og magnificently dwells."

— Clarence, poet

SACRED SITE
NEWGRANGE, BOYNE VALLEY,
IRELAND 53°69' N 6°44' W

CORRESPONDING CRYSTAL
SNOW QUARTZ

Newgrange stands on a ridge overlooking the River Boyne. More than 300,000 visitors from around the world are drawn to this place of magical mystery every year. People queue for hours to enter its immense egg-shaped chamber with its beautifully corbelled roof, particularly at the winter solstice when the Sun's light penetrates the innermost sanctuary.

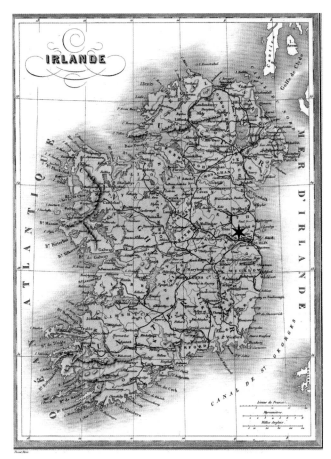

*Boyne Valley, Ireland

What this site offers you

- Deep awareness of the ancient past
- Reconnection to Irish ancestry
- Fertilization by the light of the Sun and Moon
- Renewed creativity

Crystal Connections

Quartz is often seen as sparkling specks in rocks such as Granite or in massive white seams. When excavating Newgrange, archaeologists found tons of Snow Quartz, which have been "restored" to the lower walls of the monument. The stone at Newgrange was brought in huge quantities from mountains more than 50 miles (80 km) away. The difficulty of this task shows how much the stone was prized as an energy amplifier and harvester of celestial energy. When two pieces of Snow (Milk) Quartz are rubbed together, they produce a visible spark in a dark chamber such as lies at the heart of this huge stone structure. Magical indeed.

The body of the cairn is constructed from water-tumbled pebbles 6 to 9 inches (15.2 to 22.9 cm) across and huge, natural boulders brought from the surrounding landscape. These include Greywacke, a type of Sandstone, and Slate, as well as Limestone, Granite, and other igneous rocks standing approximately 6.5 feet (2 m) high.

New Grange: The Megalithic Portal

Six thousand years ago, Irish people constructed this enormous mound, which spans more than 2 acres (0.8 ha), and some thousand years later surrounded it with a stone circle. It is known as a "passage grave," but as Anthony Murphy and Richard Moore explain in *Island of the Setting Sun*, astronomical research has shown that the site was also "a complex astronomical and calendrical device. The people who constructed it . . . could probably tell exactly what day of the year it was simply by looking at the way the sun casts shadows on the stones."

The passage within the mound bears a striking resemblance to the female reproductive organs and the site has a deep connection to the Moon. As it may have

The Newgrange mound has been refaced with Snow Quartz by archaeologists. The postholes in front delineate astronomical alignments.

been completely covered in Snow Quartz, it is suggested that the mound is an "earthly Moon." Newgrange is called the "Brugh of the Many Lights," perhaps because stellar lights shine down its length. Although Brugh is often translated "mansion," the old Irish word Bru means "womb." Brú na Bóinne could mean "womb of the bright cow" or "womb of the Moon." At the time of Newgrange's construction, the Milky Way, the "road of the illumined cow," appeared as a band around the horizon. The stream of celestial "milk" was mirrored by the river curving around the sinuous white Quartz wall of the monument: "the path of the Moon" manifested on Earth.

A pyramid-shaped stone once stood in the center of the main chamber. With a little imagination, it is possible to believe that this stone fertilized the Earth in an act of cosmological magic, when the Sun rising during the heart of midwinter pierced the cosmic egg in the Moon's womb.

Newgrange is part of a larger complex that mirrors the sky. Researchers suggest the color of the winter solstice sunrise inspired a neighboring mound's name: Red Mountain. Anthony Murphy recommends we picture a full moon rising over the hill of the Red Mountain and shining on the earthly equivalent of the Milky Way: the Boyne River. Equally, we can picture that Sun rising,

The triple spirals on the entrance stones have astronomical significance. The lightbox is above the doorway.

rimming the hill with fire, then bursting into the sky to shine life-giving rays into the dark heart of the mound at midwinter. It is a moment of singular fusion of Earth with sky.

Sunset on the same day falls over a distant hill, Realtoge, meaning "young star." Given the mythological memories of the dead being taken to Newgrange, it might also have been the moment when, as light withdrew from the chamber, the souls of the dead passed from the grave mound to return to their home in the stars.

ARCHAEOASTRONOMY

Just after nine o'clock on the morning of the winter solstice, the rays of the rising Sun enter the light box above the doorway of Newgrange. For the next seventeen minutes, a beam of light slowly creeps down the sinuous passageway until it reaches the heart of the monument. The beam conveys the fertilizing rays of the Sun into the depths of darkness to touch the standing stones. Having lit up the chamber, the narrow beam slowly retreats. The precise alignment of the light box means that ancient astronomers could accurately predict the solstice.

At midwinter sunrise, light floods down the interior passage from the light box over the door.

sinuous passageway mirrors the cruciform shape of this constellation. Just as with the Newgrange passage, the stars are slightly out of alignment. The constellation of Cygnus appears to glide along the Milky Way and slowly maps the procession of the equinox as it turns around the wheel of the year. "The giant swan appears to fly along an astral river." At this latitude today, the circumpolar star Deneb, one of Cygnus's major stars, never sets below the horizon, remaining visible all year. But when Newgrange was built, Deneb would have sat on the horizon, briefly dipping below it to set due north and then rising again like a swan taking off into the night sky.

MYTHOLOGY, LEGENDS, AND LORE

The Tuatha Dé Danann (mythical founders of the Irish) erected Newgrange as a burial place for their chief, Dagda Mór, and his three sons. Other myths credit Newgrange as the burial place of Lugh Lámhfada (Lugh of the Long Arm), spiritual father of the great mythical hero Cúchulainn who was magically conceived at Newgrange when his mother dreamed of being visited in the night by the god of light.

Newgrange offered hospitality to many guests and provided an unlimited supply of ale. Three trees were perpetually in fruit. One pig was always cooked and ready to eat while another one was alive. Newgrange had more than a touch of the supernatural about it. Another chieftain, Oengus, brought the body of his son, Diarmaid, here to "put an aeriel life into him so that he will talk to me every day."

In a myth linked to Cygnus, the god Aonghus fell in love with Caer, a maiden who visited him while he slept. After a long search Caer was located, but her father explained that she came from Sídh Uamhain, an "Otherworld [stellar] residence" in Connacht. The girl took the form of both a maiden and a swan, switching at Samhain. When Aonghus found her, she was a beautiful white swan. The pair flew off to live at Newgrange together. Even today, Whooper Swans migrate from Iceland each year to winter on the river below Newgrange.

Every nine years, however, the Moon occupies the Sun's summer and winter solstice position. Moonlight, too, enters the light box and illuminates the chamber. At certain periods during Venus's eight-year cycle, the planet is visible to anyone sitting within the chamber.

The petroglyph-carved megaliths around the mound provide a sophisticated map of significant stellar events. At the winter solstice, the shadow of a megalith at the entrance crosses the lower part of the three spirals on the west side of the curbstone. At the equinox a shadow goes through the center of the three.

Murphy and Moore have suggested that the ancients used the constellation of Cygnus, the swan, to accurately chart the night passage toward the solstice. The

Snow Quartz

Purification: Snow Quartz

Snow Quartz is the opaque, white form of Quartz. Neolithic peoples prized this stone as it stored Moon power. This gentle healing, calming, revitalizing stone takes you deep into yourself to access the ancient wisdom at your core.

SNOW QUARTZ'S PROPERTIES

The most abundant crystal on the planet, Snow Quartz energizes the soul and helps it on its journey home. This stone lets you know your true self. Snow Quartz is an integral component in rocks placed in ancient stone circles, tombs, and megalithic portals that connect to the stars and universal energy. One of its most important properties is purification. Snow Quartz has a slower frequency than clear Quartz. In ancient sites it not only amplified Earth energies, but it also stored light until required for ceremonies and rituals.

An enhancer of psychic abilities, Quartz made ancient people more receptive to metaphysical forces. Long prized for its ability to unlock memory, it was traditionally a medicine stone of great power—American Indians placed it in the cradles of newborns to signify their connection to the Earth. Australian Aborigines ingested it as part of their initiation rituals. This stone eases you into the flow of universal energy that is so much a part of indigenous ritual practice.

SNOW QUARTZ'S HEALING POWER

This master healing stone removes blockages of all kinds and gently dissolves emotional angst. It slowly brings about healing and transformation, strengthening the immune system and balancing the body. It calms an overactive mind and clears extraneous thoughts.

CONNECTING WITH SNOW QUARTZ

Holding Snow Quartz connects you not only to Newgrange but also to the many sacred sites around the world that incorporate it. The "brain cells of Mother Earth," its seams run across all continents and under the seas, stitching the planet together.

Entering the Womb

This journey takes you into the heart of Newgrange and into the womb of the Earth, to be fertilized by the light of the stellar luminaries and to meet the ancestors.

PREPARATION

Purify your crystal and ensure that you will not be disturbed. Respectfully request permission to connect to this site. Before you start, focus on the pictures of Newgrange until you can close your eyes and still see the entrance and the passageway. A Celtic or Gaelic drumming CD played in the background enhances this experience.

THE JOURNEY

Hold your crystal and breathe gently, bringing your attention deep into yourself. Close your eyes and look up at the point above and between your eyebrows. Feel your third eye open.

In your mind's eye, picture yourself standing in front of the entrance to Newgrange. Your crystal sparkles, giving you sufficient light to see. Follow the passageway deep into the mound. When you reach the end, turn and face the entrance. Sit comfortably. Place your crystal on the ground in front of you and let its light dim. All is dark. You are deep in the womb of rebirth.

Feel the silence in this ancient place and the sense of expectancy. The spirits of the ancestors are all around you. You hear a drum beating, the sound echoing off the walls. Suddenly, the end of the passage lights up with a silver glow. A faint beam makes its slow, sinuous way down the passage to the crystal, which lights up, absorbing the energy of the Moon. It touches you gently. Then the beam slowly retreats.

Again you wait. Much knowledge is gained in this dark space where the ancestors teach you their ancient wisdom.

Suddenly, the drum beats louder, more urgently. The entranceway glows with golden light. The Sun's beam rushes toward you, into your heart and mind, illuminating your spirit. For a long moment, it pauses and then it begins to recede.

Again you wait. The world turns, the Sun sinks.

Through the entrance portal, you see a faint gleam of starlight. Venus is rising. Pick up your crystal, place it just below your navel, and prepare for rebirth. Walk out of the womb, down the birth passage, and into the star's light. Focus your gaze on Venus. Hold up your crystal so that it, too, is fertilized by the starlight. Place the crystal to your heart and know that you are reborn.

When ready, bring your attention back into the room and place your crystal where you see it often. Imagine a bubble of protection wrapped around you and feel your connection to the Earth.

Alternative Crystals

Granite was traditionally used to create megalithic portals.

Grey Granite

Chapter 12

THE
HEART CHAKRA
OF THE WORLD

— GLASTONBURY —

*"Glastonbury is a gateway to the Unseen. It has been a holy place and
pilgrim-way from time immemorial, and to this day it sends its ancient call into
the heart of the race it guards, and still we answer to the inner voice."*

—**Dion Fortune**, Avalon of the Heart

SACRED SITE
GLASTONBURY, SOMERSET,
ENGLAND 51°09' N 2°43' W

CORRESPONDING CRYSTAL
AMMONITE

At one time, Glastonbury stood tall above encircling
marshes, in a shining sea. The Tor, healing well, sacred tree,
and Abbey ruins are today enfolded within a landscape zodiac
that may have been trodden by Christ himself. Tradition says
he came here three times as a child. In the pagan view of the
world, Avalon was where the dead went to the Otherworld.
Glastonbury is an interconnection of sacred sites from different
traditions that creates one numinous whole. The spiral of an
Ammonite mirrors the labyrinth that winds it way up the Tor.

* Glastonbury, England

What this site offers you

- Heart-centeredness
- Entrance into the Earth's heart chakra
- Strength in your chakra system and the Earth's
- Connection to landscape energies
- Understanding of the vast cycles of time
- Acceptance of change and evolution
- Access to the continuity of all life

Crystal Connections

Ammonites are everywhere in Glastonbury, as this area was underwater for millions of years. These ancient sea creatures died and were fossilized, only to surface when the land was drained. The Abbey is constructed of fossilized limestone, the Chalice Well Gardens' soil has an abundance of it, and the Tor is underpinned with them. Nearby Dulcote Quarry reveals wonderful "pudding stones," Agate nodules that open to reveal Calcite, Geothite, and, if you are extremely fortunate, Amethyst interiors.

Glastonbury: Avalon of the Heart

Otherworldly and mystical, Avalon exists in a parallel dimension to Glastonbury and is seen through the inner eye of vision. Here the Grail resides, the legendary cup of Christ that has much older connotations. Avalon is the numinous heart of this landscape, the etheric chamber of the heart chakra of the world.

Glastonbury Tor was home to Gwyn ap Nudd, king of the Fair Folk and lord of the Underworld. It is where King Arthur lies awaiting the call to rise again and bring England to glory. Considerable mythological evidence exists for the presence of this king at Avalon. As Dion Fortune said, "the Tor is indeed the Hill of Vision for any whose eyes have the least inclination to open upon another world."

St Michael's tower glimpsed through a misty morning on the Tor.

Chalice Well cover designed by Bligh Bond.

THE TOR AND THE LABYRINTH

Now dominated by the tower of a ruined church that was cast down in an earthquake in 1275, the Tor was once crowned by a stone circle, a Temple to the Sun. It is still an extraordinary experience to stand on the Tor at full Moon and see the setting Sun slowly sink into the west as the Moon majestically rises in the east. Sunrise and sunset on the old English folk festivals of Beltane (May 1) and Lughnasadh or Lammas (August 1) align along the axis of the Tor.

The Tor church was dedicated to Saint Michael, the archangel of fire who stands on a serpent. In Christian tradition, Michael was the dragon slayer who threw down the old pagan gods. Before Christianity, the Tor was perceived as an enormous dragon lying in the landscape. Around the Tor winds a huge, multidimensional, serpentine labyrinth, an ancient processional way. Labyrinths and spirals were traditionally part of goddess worship, symbolizing the soul's journey through birth, death, and rebirth.

ALCHEMICAL MARRIAGE: THE RED AND WHITE SPRINGS

Glastonbury's Red and White Springs once flowed freely, one from deep within the Tor itself, the other from the foot of adjoining Chalice Hill, until they mingled in a sacred stream: the Brue. As Dion Fortune says, this site was sacred to the old gods and their dark powers, and she suggests that the well was the magic mirror of Morgan le Fay. Pupil of the legendary magician Merlin, Morgan wove spells around her brother Arthur to ensnare him. Later, Chalice Hill was the mythical home of the Fisher King of Arthurian legend, who suffered eternally from a grievous wound in whose heart he kept the Grail.

Iron stains the Chalice Well spring deep red, and the water looks like magical blood. Calcium deposits keep the White Spring clear. The two form an alchemical marriage. The eternally renewing phoenix, symbol of Aquarius in the Glastonbury zodiac (explained later), springs from this spot drinking the water of life from the well.

The Glastonbury Thorn, surrounded by "sacred litter," with the Tor in the distance.

Below the Vesica Piscis cover, designed by metaphysician Bligh Bond in the early twentieth century, lies an ancient stone chamber large enough to hold a standing man. Its three sides were hollowed from a single piece of Sarsen stone carried many miles to this place. A sluice gate enables it to be emptied and refilled. Many people believe this was an initiation chamber for rebirth mysteries. Others believe that a Grail cup was found here. As the Sun rises over the Tor on the summer solstice, a shaft of light penetrates the well chamber and touches the heart of anyone who stands there.

MYTHOLOGY, LEGENDS, AND LORE

"The poetry of the soul writes itself in Glastonbury."

Dion Fortune, metaphysician and author

Glastonbury has been a center of pilgrimage since time immemorial. It is believed that the Druids had a university here. The labyrinth on the Tor is reputedly Neolithic. Glastonbury was one of the earliest Christian sites in England. Myths and legends abound about this holy place and the major British ley line—the intertwined Michael and Mary line—passes through its center. Tradition tells us Joseph of Arimathea was a tin trader who came to Glastonbury bringing the young Jesus with him.

THE HOLY GRAIL

According to legend, after the death of Christ, Joseph of Arimathea brought to Glastonbury the cup used at the Last Supper in which he had caught a few drops of the sacred blood. In a dream, he was told to gather twelve disciples and sail toward the setting sun. Upon reaching Glastonbury, he founded the earliest Christian church. An Abbey chapel featured a zodiac-patterned floor with the Sun in the center, a reference to the twelve companions of Saint Joseph. The cup stood on the altar of the Abbey, but later the Grail was given into the keeping of the Fisher King at the Chalice Well.

THE GLASTONBURY THORN

It's said that when Joseph of Arimathea landed at Wearyall Hill, he stuck his staff in the ground and from it sprouted the Holy Thorn, which blossomed immediately even though it was midwinter. The thorn is a type found only in the Levant and it flowers at Christmas. Cut down in the Reformation, a slip took root. Although recently cut down by vandals, the tree sprouted again after being given healing by local pagans with the blessing of the local vicar. An offshoot of the Holy Thorn grows in the Abbey grounds. Wearyall Hill forms the northern fish of Pisces in the Glastonbury zodiac.

THE ABBEY

Glastonbury Abbey was one of the greatest religious houses in Britain, due in no small part to its claim that the legendary King Arthur and his Queen Guinevere were buried close to its high altar. The grave can still be seen today. Thousands of people made pilgrimages to this holy site until the Dissolution of the Monasteries by Henry VIII.

At one of my favorite places in Glastonbury, the Retreat House in Chilkwell Street where I run annual astrological retreats, the Mary line exits through the former gatehouse of the Abbey. A cross with two cruets, the coat of arms of Joseph of Arimathea, adorns one side of the gate. According to legend, one cruet was gold and held the blood of Christ, the other was silver and held his sweat—an alchemical wedding of male

The Gateway to Abbey House

and female reflecting the Michael and Mary line. On the other side of the gateway is a carving of a dragon. This place is the tail of the phoenix in the Glastonbury zodiac. I can attest it is an extremely potent place for entering expanded consciousness.

THE MICHAEL AND MARY LINE

The great dragon ley line of southern England, the Michael and Mary Earth-energy line intertwines across the landscape from St. Michael's Mount in Cornwall to Hopton on the Suffolk coast, passing across the greatest width of England. It runs through many churches dedicated to St. Michael and the Virgin Mary or Mary Magdalene. Crossing standing stones, dolmens, and the enormous stone circle at Avebury, the line is orientated to Beltane (May Day) sunrise. In earlier times, fires were lit along the whole line on Beltane. A watcher would have seen the Sun suddenly blaze up from beyond the line of beacon fires. The cosmological union of earthly fire and celestial sun was repeated at Lughnasadh (August 1).

The lines cross at three places in Glastonbury: the Abbey, Chalice Well, and the Tor. They merge just behind the grave of King Arthur and his queen, a powerful alchemical marriage point.

The Zodiacal Giants of Somerset correspond with the Stars of their respective Celestial Constellations.

THE GLASTONBURY ZODIAC

In the 1920s, Katherine Maltwood plotted a landscape zodiac around Glastonbury. Landscape zodiacs map the ecliptic, the Sun's path, and vast zodiacal constellations set out on the land. They are the physical, earthly counterpart of the celestial sky: fulfilling the aphorism "as above, so below." Two great dogs guard the zodiac and guide travelers who make a pilgrimage around the wheel.

THE WORLD CHAKRAS

"There are tides in the inner life, and on the crest of their flood, we are very near to heaven. There are times when the power-tides of the Unseen flow strongly down upon our Earth, and there are also places upon her surface where the channels are open and they come through in the fullness of power. This was known to them of old time, who had much wisdom that we have forgotten, and they availed themselves of both times and places when they sought to awaken the higher consciousness."

Dion Fortune

Energy vortex points around the world carry Earth energy through a subtle meridian grid interspersed with vortices. These vortices correspond to the chakras on the human body. The Earth's chakras link sacred sites around the globe through complex sacred geometry. These chakras cover many miles, radiating out from a central point. Not all authorities agree on exactly where or how many of these chakras exist, but most agree that Glastonbury is Earth's heart chakra.

Earth Chakra	Site
Base	Mount Shasta, California (alternatives: Grand Canyon, Sedona, Black Mesa)
Sacral	Lake Titicaca, South America (alternatives: Machu Picchu, Amazon River)
Solar plexus	Uluru, Australia
Heart	Glastonbury, England (alternative: River Ganges, India)
Throat	Great Pyramid, Egypt
Third eye	Kuh-e Malek Siah, Iran (alternative: Mount Fuji, Japan)
Crown	Mount Kailash, Tibet

Vortices are aligned to elemental forces: earth, air, fire, and water. A rainbow serpent or dragon current links them. Additional Earth chakras are being activated to assimilate higher vibrational energies. Earth-healing ceremonies at the chakras and other vortex points open, purify, align, and heal the Earth's energy field and maintain overall global wellbeing.

THE FOUR ELEMENTAL VORTICES

Elemental Vortices	Site
Earth	Table Mountain, Cape Town, South Africa
Air	Mount of Olives, Jerusalem, Israel
Fire	Haleakala Crater, Hawaii, United States
Water	Lake Rotopounamu, New Zealand

Ammonite

The Cauldron of Wisdom: Ammonite

Ancient life-forms solidified into fossils such as Ammonite. A symbol of stability, Ammonite has been a protective talisman and wisdom keeper for thousands of years. Its form takes you deep inside yourself or lets you explore the multidimensions of consciousness. This stone links to the goddess and the slow, expanding spirals of evolution.

AMMONITE'S PROPERTIES

This stone's gently flowing spiral of energy helps you come full circle and find your essence, the true shape of your soul. It invokes a powerful connection between your heart and that of Mother Earth. Ammonite assists in traveling through time and space to explore the distant past, the immensity of the present, or the far future. Used to strengthen the personal or planetary chakra system, it activates metaphysical abilities. Placed over the soma chakra, it stimulates out-of-body journeying; over the third eye, psychic sight; over the heart, infinite compassion. On the sacral chakra it stimulates mystic feminine creativity, and on the base chakra it helps kundalini power to rise. This stone of personal empowerment has your soul's path encoded within it.

AMMONITE'S HEALING POWER

Excellent for anything that needs structure, Ammonite is particularly helpful for healing birth trauma. This powerful karmic cleanser gently peels away layers of the past to let you perceive your true self. It releases obsessions and mental imperatives and stimulates your survival instincts. Encouraging a strong flow of Qi, Ammonite reframes cellular memory, assisting cell metabolism and switching on beneficial genetic potential. It helps overcome degenerative conditions.

CONNECTING WITH AMMONITE

Meditating with Ammonite takes you deep into your own heart and that of the Earth and its energetic chakra system.

Meditation: Moving into the Heart

With your eyes closed, use your finger to trace the spiral of your Ammonite toward the center. Tell yourself you are in the heart chakra of the world, ascending the spiral around the Tor. When you get to the center, feel the beating heart of Mother Earth coming to you through the connection of the crystal with the Tor. Feel how it resonates within your own heart as the beats synchronize.

When you put down the Ammonite, your heart remains connected to Mother Earth's.

Alternative Stones

Opalized Ammolite (a type of Ammonite) from North America can be substituted for Limestone. Or, use Dulcote Pudding Stone, a local Agate-with-Calcite found a few miles from the Tor.

Ammolite

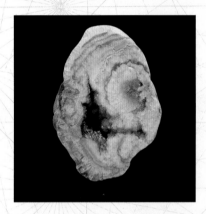

Dulcote Pudding Stone

Limestone

Chapter 13

IN THE
FOOTSTEPS
OF THE ANCESTORS

— STONEHENGE AND THE PRESELI MOUNTAINS —

"The very act of bringing of stones from the far west, the ultimate reaches of the world, the borders of the Land of the Dead, the place where the sun and moon sank beneath the waves of the world [may] have validated Stonehenge as the primary source of power where all places and all spirits, all stories, all ancestors, came together and were held harmoniously within one great structure ... that fulfilled a collective dream."

— *Simon and Sue Lilly,* Preseli Bluestone

⊘ **SACRED SITES**

STONEHENGE, WILSHIRE,
ENGLAND, 51°10' N 1°49' W
AND THE PRESELI MOUNTAINS,
NORTH PEMBROKESHIRE,
WALES, 51°56' N 4°46' W

◈ **CORRESPONDING CRYSTAL**

PRESELI BLUESTONE

*T*his dual sacred site encompasses two countries, linked by a rock: Preseli Bluestone. These sites incorporate many core features of sacred landscape: geology, water, acoustics, healing, cosmology, mythology, landscape, and the elements. You can plug into the energy of these unique paired sites with the assistance of Preseli Bluestone.

Crystal Connections

Crystals form an integral part of Stonehenge. The Preseli Bluestones have their origin in Wales, as testing done by academic researchers Nick Pearce and Richard Bevins (www.archnews.co.uk) and Colin Sheering (www.britannia.com) shows, and have always been an important aspect of this megalithic henge. Bluestone has visible Feldspar inclusions that shine white like stars. The Welsh stones also feature Rhyolite Jasper, a shamanic journeying stone with powerful links to the past. Bluestone could have been revered as a cosmological sky map, a guidebook for the gods. The central "altar stone," long believed to be Bluestone, is a pale green Garnet-studded Sandstone menhir from nearby Milford Haven.

Garnet was revered for its magical and therapeutic powers of illumination and healing. Zircons embedded in the stones are being studied, but the ancients used them as protection against lightning, bodily harm, and disease, which would point to the henge's use as a healing site. But the Bluestones are the major power source at this iconic site. The stones would have been venerated for their resonant acoustic properties; they effected sound healing and induced altered states of consciousness.

Stonehenge and Preseli: United by Stone

Archaeologists are just beginning to comprehend the complex relationship between Stonehenge, land of the ancestors; nearby Durrington Walls, with its huge Chalk-covered henge and two timber post circles symbolizing the land of the living; and the river that connects them. Why the vast site is so closely connected to a Welsh mountain 135 miles (217 km) away remains a mystery to them. They are unsure why the Bluestones were brought from the Preseli Mountains, an enormous distance for Neolithic people to traverse without the wheel. Geomancers, archeoastronomers, and crystal workers can, however, throw light on this amazing feat. Recent excavations are revealing the origins of the people who built Stonehenge—perhaps in memory of their ancient sacred mountain home—and the immense age of the pre-existing sacred site.

* Preseli Mountains (North Pembrokeshire, Wales)
* Stonehenge (Wilshire, England)

What these sites offer you

- Attunes you to the sacred and the power of Mother Earth
- Opportunity to sit in the womb of time
- Personal or planetary healing
- Reconnection to the ancestors
- Expanded awareness
- Knowledge of past wisdom and skills
- Insight into your purpose in incarnating
- An opportunity to offer service to the Earth

Bluestone outcrop on the top of the Preseli Mountains.

The stones encompass a potent mix of crystal energies to seed into the surrounding landscape and to facilitate shamanic rituals at the site. They embody the ancient Welsh word *hiraeth*, a deep longing for reconnection with the spiritual homeland and the ancestors.

> *"Hiraeth is in the mountains where the wind speaks in many tongues and the buzzards fly on silent wings. It's the call of my spiritual home, it's where ancient peoples made their home . . . Hiraeth—the link with the long-forgotten past, the language of the soul, the call from the inner self. Half forgotten—fractionally remembered. It speaks from the rocks, from the earth, from the trees and in the waves. It's always there. Yes, I hear it."*
>
> *Val Bethell, Hiraeth, Wales Arts, www.bbc.co.uk*

You, too, can share this hiraeth, this reconnection to the spiritual power of the sacred ancestral lands, by journeying with Bluestones. If you have Celtic ancestry, it connects you to your distant past. Bluestones also provide a powerful connection with Earth energies, facilitating healing and living in harmony with our planet.

WHY LINK THE TWO SITES?

Plant the acoustic, resonant healing properties of the Preseli Mountains into the Salisbury Plain Chalk, and what do you get? A power battery that you can still plug into today through Bluestone. This linking may have been part of an extremely ancient tradition that encompassed the animistic concept of landscape—and rocks in particular—being alive and imbued with a spirit of place. Anthropologists are familiar with this concept, and not only so-called primitive tribes take this view. The same belief holds in Japan today, where Bluestone is particularly venerated by crystal workers. In moving the stones, migrating Celts took their deities and their sacred homeland with them.

> *"Archaeologists are aware that rocks from natural places that were venerated were circulated over considerable distances in the Neolithic era of prehistory. These 'pieces of place' were, in effect, relics charged with the sanctity, the* mana, *of their homeland, much as the bones of saints that were circulated and venerated in Medieval times were thought to possess magical and healing qualities."*
>
> S.P.A.C.E.S., "A Stone Age Holy Land?"
> *www.landscape-perception.com*

Asking "what besides their color made these Bluestones so special?" the academics working with the Strumble Preseli Ancient Communities and Environment Study came to the conclusion that sound—the resonant quality of Bluestones—combined with water may have been a core reason why the Preseli outcrop was venerated by Stone Age people and why stones were relocated when they migrated south.

But crystal workers will tell you that the unique electromagnetic frequencies of the Bluestones themselves are healing and fortifying, creating a natural gem essence as the water passed through the rock and into the surrounding springs. As Sue and Simon Lilly, who reintroduced me to this amazing stone, say in *Preseli Bluestone: Healing Stone of the Ancestors,* if the virtues of Preseli Bluestone could be summed up in one phrase it would be that it 'anchors body, mind and spirit in an expanded horizon of awareness.' Geomancers attest that Preseli and Stonehenge are places of potent Earth energies like no other, energies that are locked into the rocks and crystals at their core. Rock was Stone Age people's technology, and it may have been far more sophisticated than the relics left behind would, at first glance, suggest.

The Crystal Source: Mynydd Preseli (the Preseli Mountains)

Compasses go crazy in the Preseli Mountains, particularly at Carn Menyn where Stonehenge's Bluestones were sourced. It was revered as a healing site for thousands of years, as archaeology and mythology attest. The whole site is riddled with geomagnetic anomalies and powerful telluric currents, adding power to the stones. More than 300 elliptical stone circles with astronomical alignments exist, along with graves, cairns, prehistoric rock art, sight lines, and healing springs that were visited at least eight thousand years before Christ.

In this immensely old landscape, the power of the gods and the elements is instantly visible. Stand atop the ridge and watch a storm roll in from the sea; be encompassed in cloud and mist, lashed with wind and driving rain, and you know the power of nature in all its awesome rawness—as you do when the fiery Sun shines again and a rainbow bridges the heavens with the Earth.

This unique rock offers itself up. It splits into neat megaliths that need no further working, other than planting them into the Earth to transmit its power. The name of the local village, Maenclochog, means "clamourous stones." It has been demonstrated that the 110 Hz primary sound band, to which the stones resonate, has powerful effects on the human brain, producing profound trance states. Devereux and Wozencroft, who have been researching the acoustics at Preseli, suggest,

> *"Preseli may have been the sacred destination of pilgrimages, possibly linked with the ritual, sacramental use of psilocybin mushrooms—and we can imagine that in bemushroomed visionary states the ringing of the rocks may have taken on magical dimensions, even causing the spirits in the stones to appear and dance before stoned Stone Age eyes."*

As a natural psychic who has stood on Carn Menyn in the atmospheric prelude to a thunderstorm, I can attest that you don't need to be stoned to see the stones dance. The wind that howls through the rocks produces hauntingly eerie flutelike music that takes you into an altered state. The rocks themselves give off electrostatic energy that shimmers so powerfully, the whole place appears ready to lift off at any moment. To be there is to dance with the ancients in a place of preternatural connection.

MYTHOLOGY, LEGENDS, AND LORE

In the Preseli Mountains lies the entrance to the Celtic Underworld, Annwn. Welsh folklore regards the area as the gateway to the Underworld and as being of particular significance to Merlin and the Druids. The area appears repeatedly in Arthurian legend. Such folktales, although superimposed onto more recent historical times, carry with them the resonance of ancient stories of magic and daring.

Modern folk belief in Pembrokeshire says that the Bluestones and the springs around their base possess healing qualities. Magic mushrooms are gathered by those who wish to experience ancestral and spiritual visions.

The Womb of Time: Stonehenge

Perhaps the most iconic sacred site, Stonehenge rises out of the Salisbury Plain like a mountain. Hardly surprising, as archaeology is proving that the early stone builders of Stonehenge came here from the sacred Preseli Mountains, as did the Bluestones. The stones symbolized the womb of time for ancient Britons with their connection to the ancestors.

The Bluestones are now arranged in a horseshoe inside the Sarsen-stone outer ring. The arrangement mimics the Preseli landscape, where the central outcrop of Carn Menyn has Dolerite and Rhyolite, with tuff rocks around its fringe. Bluestone was once the only stone at Stonehenge, forming an outer ring known as the Aubrey Holes. The whole site was shining white with exposed Chalk. Plugging a Bluestone into Chalk creates a battery that amplifies natural Earth currents on the Plain and in the water that flows beneath the circle in a spiral formation. As the stones were resonant and hollowed out; it also created a natural musical instrument whose sound added to the atmosphere of this site. It produced an altered state of consciousness in people who participated in the ceremonies.

A place of the ancestors for thousands of years, Stonehenge was the center for burial rites. It was also a surprisingly accurate calendar and, legend has it, a potent source of healing as well. It attracted not just locals but people from Europe and farther away. One of the most significant archaeological finds was the grave of "the Amesbury Archer," a skilled metalworker who traveled from the Swiss Alps in 2300 BCE when the stones were being realigned into the site we know today. His grave contained intricately crafted gold objects, the earliest found in Britain. Metalworkers were the wonder workers of their time—they knew the secrets of alchemically transforming rock into molten metal with the magical element of fire, and of casting sacred and profane objects. That the Archer was attracted to Stonehenge reveals its reputation throughout the ancient world. That he had been gravely wounded, but that his fractures were healed suggests a reason for his presence at this sacred site—low-level magnetic fields stimulate rapid healing for broken bones.

IN THE BEGINNING

Archaeological evidence suggested that Stonehenge began around 8000 BCE when the site was cleared of trees and an avenue constructed down to the river—although recent research has pushed the date back even further. Natural parallel depressions running across the Chalk surface of the land are exactly aligned to midwinter sunrise and would have held ice that shone in the early morning light—a magical pointer to rebirth at the winter solstice. Postholes aligned east–west suggest that huge wooden poles were erected there, marking the spring and autumn equinoxes—an alignment that was reconstructed several times over the following millennia.

For almost a thousand years before the stones arrived at the site, a wooden temple marked this spot. Over the next 2,000 years, it slowly evolved into the huge trilithon-dominated circle we see today. Around 3000 BCE, a ditch and henge were constructed, along with

The Bluestones in situ in their "new" home, the central circle of Stonehenge.

the Aubrey Holes that mapped the Moon's cycle. Evidence is emerging that the Bluestones were originally located in these holes. At this time, the two parallel entry stones were aligned to the midsummer solstice sunrise. A thousand years later, the Bluestones were realigned to the summer solstice. The famous lintel-linked Sarsen-stone circle was the last phase to be completed and the Bluestones were again relocated, this time to the center.

ORIGINS OF THE BUILDERS

Scientific analysis of bones excavated from graves in the area of Stonehenge reveals that the builders themselves originated in Preseli. Did migrating ancient Celts seek an already-sacred site to plant their healing-magic stones? Or did the Druids of Stonehenge send for the Bluestones because of their reputation and that of Preseli itself? We'll probably never know, but a potent fusion of knowledge and power occurred, and these two sites remain energetically linked to this day.

MYTHOLOGY, LEGENDS, AND LORE

Stonehenge legends abound. It was the mythological home of Druids, the magical astronomer–priests of old. Geoffrey of Monmouth, who created much of the mythology around King Arthur, tells us in his medieval *Historia Regium Britanniae* that Merlin, King Arthur's magician, flew the stones to Stonehenge from a circle in Ireland—the site of a small Bluestone outcrop. The legend encapsulates a mythological truth of change and transformation and points to the importance of magic in the ancient world. Geoffrey states that the stones had medicinal properties that could be accessed by washing the stones and then pouring the water into baths—modern crystal workers make crystal essences the same way.

A powerful energetic connection runs between Preseli and Stonehenge through the Earth's magnetic grid. Myth says sound aided the stones' flight to Stonehenge. Bluestone is a highly electromagnetic and acoustically resonant material. Modern scientists have produced small antigravity machines that use electromagnetic and sonic levitation. It is tempting to think that they have rediscovered a power known to our ancient ancestors.

ARCHAEOASTRONOMY

The evidence from observatories such as Stonehenge that Neolithic peoples had a fully formed cosmology and recognized the cycles of the seasons, Sun, Moon, planets, and stars is compelling. Before the stone circle was built, the 6-feet (1.8 m)-high bank made a perfect viewing platform from which to observe the heavens, a kind of Stone Age planetarium. A false horizon gives the best view of the rising and setting of stellar bodies.

The earliest wooden pillars were probably equinoctial siting poles for the astronomical alignment of the spring and autumn equinoxes. Such poles could also have been seen as drawing the power of the Sun down to Earth. Once the stones themselves were erected, mapping and capturing further astronomical alignments, the site became even more awesome as the Sun's light was condensed into an intense ray of solar energy that penetrated the heart of the circle at an important turning point of the year.

Uniquely around the latitude of Stonehenge, the most northerly midsummer solstice sunrise and the most northerly standstill Moon set, which occurs every 18.6 years and is known as the nodal cycle of the Moon, occur at right angles to each other, and the same is true for the southerly midwinter solstice sunset and standstill moonrise.

The most famous astronomical alignment at Stonehenge is undoubtedly the midsummer sunrise over the Heelstone, creating a shaft of light that penetrates the huge trilithon circle. Take yourself back in time and imagine standing in the darkness of predawn surrounded by towering, ringing stones at that magical moment when the Sun blazed in full glory. Even today, this is a stunning event. A shaman standing on this axis with his hands thrown up to greet the Sun would have appeared supernaturally illuminated by an aureole of light. Larger than life, he was imbued with awesome power. Think, too, how it might have felt at midwinter when the slowly dying Sun was reborn anew.

Nearby Woodhenge is similarly aligned to the midsummer sunrise, while the allied site, Durrington Walls, was aligned to midwinter sunrise. Archaeological evidence suggests feasting and ceremony occurred here in the dead of winter when the ashes and bones of the departed were gathered for their journey down the river to the land of the ancestors. The winter solstice marked a point of hope—rebirth of light, heat, and fertility for the coming year. The two henges show the physical transition from wooden henges at Durrington, in the land of the newly dead and the still living, into stone, the enduring place of the ancestors. They indicate the importance of stone's qualities for those ancient people.

Now imagine how the ancients felt when the Sun or Moon "died" during an eclipse. Anyone who has witnessed a total solar eclipse knows how awe-inspiring it is as day turns to night, birdsong ceases, the world grows still, and darkness sweeps over the land. Even today, you watch with trepidation. Will light ever return? Equally impressive is the eclipse of the Moon as it slowly turns blood red while being consumed by a dark shadow. Surely, ceremonies would be needed to propitiate the gods and bring light back to Earth? The Aubrey Holes, mapped the phases of the 18.6 year nodal Moon cycle and its eclipses, so that preparations could be made for such ceremonies.

ARCHAEOACOUSTICS

The science of archaeoacoustics is still in its infancy, but it is being applied to sacred sites around the world by Jon Wozencroft and Paul Devereux (www.landscape-perception.com) and is producing soundscapes that have incredible effects on human consciousness. Imagine standing inside an enormous drum, feeling the percussive vibrations passing through your whole body. Consider the effect on your mind. Now add the chanting of the human voice. Picture the powerful reverberation of a medieval cathedral during the sonorous Latin Mass because, in essence, this is the Stonehenge experience.

Stonehenge would have reverberated with the sound waves of ceremonies enacted there for worship, entreaty, or healing. The Sarsen stones are hollowed out in such a way as to enhance sound's movement through the passages, echoing off the massive stones, creating overtones and harmonies. Bluestones at the site sound like a drum or ring like a gong when struck. The vibrations would have heightened both the drama and the psychospiritual effect of ritual.

Preseli Bluestone (Spotted Dolerite)

This unique Dolorite occurs naturally in only two locations: Preseli in Pembrokeshire, Wales, and a small outcropping in Ireland. Preseli Bluestone helps you connect to Earth energies and the wisdom of Celtic and Druidic peoples.

PRESELI BLUESTONE'S PROPERTIES

Bluestone from the Preseli Mountains in Wales is unique. It has high paramagnetic resonance and a distinctive appearance: blue with prominent white spots when it is wet or freshly cut. Recognized for thousands of years, its healing power is palpable. Holding this stone aligns you to Stonehenge, Earth's meridian grid, and esoteric knowledge.

Bluestone reconnects you to your ancient knowing, helping you live in harmony with the Earth and everything on it. It expands your senses, taking you beyond the mundane and into the metaphysical realms where perception is sharper and wider. You see the world with different eyes when you connect to Bluestone and its sacred sites. Carrying immense healing energy and forming a doorway to other dimensions, Bluestone helps you access the past or future when you place it on the soma chakra midway along the hairlines, or base of the skull. It links you to the magical, archetypal Merlin energy that brings out the shaman in everyone and is excellent for multidimensional journeying.

Bluestone

Preseli Bluestone has an ancient connection to the ancestors and to the cosmos. It contains strong magnetic currents—to touch the rock is, for sensitive people, a kinesthetic experience. Bluestone gives off a palpable electromagnetic charge: you literally feel a spark, especially at the site itself. Some people feel comfortable with the stone, others uncomfortable, and some feel nothing at all. This may be due to the vibrations of the stone matching or mismatching the frequency of a person's biomagnetic field (the aura). The magnetic current imprinted into the stone needs to be properly aligned. If you feel nothing, or if a headache develops when you use Bluestone, turn yourself or the stone so that the stone's magnetic resonance aligns with the cardinal points of the Earth. This facilitates healing or journeying with the stone.

BLUESTONE'S HEALING POWER

Bluestone is strongly connected to the telluric, or dragon, currents of the Earth, which spiral out from the Preseli Mountains. This current can be harnessed for personal and Earth healing, and to access ancient knowledge. Holding Bluestone increases your sensitivity to vibrations and heightens your awareness of crystal, meridian, or sound frequencies. It opens your metaphysical senses.

By balancing the meridians and restoring energetic harmony, Bluestone creates core stability for the physical and energetic bodies. Stones with magnetic fields have been demonstrated to stimulate rapid healing of broken bones. Placed over the thymus (higher heart chakra) Bluestone strengthens the psychic immune system. At the base of the skull, it harmonizes the brain stem and activates the hippocampus, an inner compass that helps orient you in the physical world. Combining Bluestone with Chalk produces a powerful battery to combat energy depletion in the physical body or the Earth.

CONNECTING WITH PRESELI BLUESTONE

Harness the power of Bluestone by meditating with it or wearing it to attune to its healing resonance. This revitalizes your biomagnetic field and brings your chakras and all the subtle bodies into balance. A balanced biomagnetic field leads to a feeling of well-being and cessation of dis-ease. Carrying Bluestone with you activates your inner compass so that you always travel in the right direction.

Alternative Stone

There really is no alternative to Bluestone for this journey. You can easily obtain one via the Internet.

The Bluestone Journey

Experience the power of the numinous and reconnect to Mother Earth, link to these ancient sites and to their power of personal and Earth healing with this journeying meditation. It puts you in touch with ancient healing power that revitalizes you and stimulates your creativity and your enthusiasm. You can return this healing energy to the Earth as an act of service to the planet in its time of need. The journey also accesses Druidic wisdom, reconnects to your previous lives in the Celtic world, and reclaims the knowledge you find there.

PREPARATION

Before undertaking the journey, respectfully request permission to connect to the sites and ensure that you will not be disturbed. Switch off the phone, and wrap yourself in a blanket. Lying down makes it easier to place the crystal, but comfort is more important than position. A drumming CD helps you move into an altered state of consciousness. Orientate yourself north–south or east–west, depending on the magnetic alignment of your Bluestone.

THE JOURNEY

Settle yourself comfortably and close your eyes. Hold your Bluestone in your hands for a few moments while taking deep, slow breaths. As you exhale, let go of tension. As you inhale, feel yourself relaxing deeper into your connection with the stone and the Earth.

When you feel ready, place the Bluestone on the soma chakra at your hairline, just above your third eye. Without opening your eyes, look up to your third eye as this helps images to form.

Feel the stone lifting and transporting you to the Preseli Mountains, where they rise from the bedrock of their Welsh home. The Bluestone knows the way, and its powerful electromagnetic properties teleport you to the rocky outcrop at the top of the mountain. If you are visual, you may see the mountain coming into view with the sea sparkling beyond it. If you are kinesthetic (feeling orientated), you sense movement and rushing air.

Alight in front of the basin of the sacred spring. Picture dipping your hands into the healing water and drinking, then dipping your Bluestone in the water.

Sit among the rocks. Be aware of the currents and vibrations that surround you as you sit in this liminal place at the joining of two worlds: the known and the unknown. It is predawn; the Sun has not yet risen, but the sky is lightening.

As you look out over the land, you see the Earth's grid and connections to all its sacred sites spiraling out before you. If any of the lines look ragged or broken, see them magically heal themselves so that the Earth's currents flow freely again.

When you feel ready, follow the energetic path that leads southeast to Stonehenge. Let the Bluestone transport you. As you fly over the land, the River Seven shines below you. Pass over it and continue toward the stone circle on the flat, white plain which pulls you like a magnet. When you land, Stonehenge is complete, mysterious, numinous. Walk the ritual way until you reach the temple's entrance. Ask permission to enter.

Walk into the center of the shadowy temple and place your stone with its healing water on the altar stone.

Music plays as you make your way to the center of the Bluestone Horseshoe facing the Heelstone. The rocks ring. Voices sound. The people have gathered with you to greet the midsummer dawn.

Suddenly, a beam of light flashes down the center of the temple, striking you in the heart and radiating through your whole body. A roar goes up. The light of the Sun has arrived. You are fertilized, made new, healed, reborn.

When you are ready to leave, the stone brings you back to your body. The silver cord attached to your soma chakra reels you back. Settle yourself comfortably in your body. Breathe deeply, stretch your fingers and toes, and then get up slowly. Picture a bubble of protection around you. Feel the connection your feet make to the Earth. Notice how much more in tune with the Earth you feel as you walk lightly upon it, how your consciousness has expanded, and how your senses are more finely attuned to the beauty around you.

Sonia's Experience: Connecting in Depth

When doing the Bluestone journey, I was taken to a flat ridge that looked out over the countryside on a misty early morning. I was told to look to the sky, which turned black, then asked to look at the stars. It was explained to me that as long as man has walked upon this plane, we have looked to the stars and known through this visible evidence that we are not the only ones.

I was asked to look at the ground and told that *everything* naturally made has purpose for our use. My attention was drawn to the moss on the Preseli stones; it became vivid green, luminescent, almost as if I were hallucinating. The green became more and more intense, and I was able to see every microscopic detail of the plant, each single cell. The dewdrops on the moss became microscopes, and I could look deep into the plant and see every separate filament. *Everything* has this much depth, from the tiniest microscopic organism to the largest. Plants, creatures, rocks, crystals are all here for our use as medicine, food, shelter, and to enable us to access knowledge and understanding, both spiritual and material. *Everything* has a purpose for our highest use on this plane of existence.

The Sun at the summer and winter solstice was particularly significant to the builders of Stonehenge. ▶

Chapter 14

MEETING THE MOTHER OF GOD

— MEDJUGORJE —

"Medjugorje is a blessed place and a grace of God, who goes to Medjugorje returns transformed, changed, he reflects himself in that source of grace that is Christ . . . I believe that we should look at Medjugorje with serenity and trust, appreciating all the good and holy things that happen in that place."

—Cardinal Ersilio Tonini, 2009

SACRED SITE

MEDJUGORJE,
BOSNIA–HERZEGOVINA
43° 12' N 17° 41' E

CORRESPONDING CRYSTAL

BLUE QUARTZ

*T*he name *Medjugorje* means "between the hills." On June 24, 1981, six Croatian young people were playing on Crnica Hill (renamed Apparition Hill) in Medjugorje, then part of Communist Yugoslavia, when a lady appeared and spoke to them. Three days later, she told them she was Gospa, the Mother of God.

* Medjugorje, Bosnia–Herzegovina

What this site offers you

- Deep connection to Mary, the Mother of God
- Expansion into the divine feminine
- Profound peace and reconciliation with the divine

Crystal Connections

Blue Quartz is colored by various minerals, including Boulangerite, a rare mineral found near Medjugorje. This Quartz, however, was chosen for its qualities and spiritual connection rather than the geology of the country. Many pilgrims pick up stones from Apparition Hill to use as links.

Compassionate Blue Quartz helps you understand your spiritual nature—it is useful if you are going through any kind of metamorphosis. It inspires hope and fires your creativity. Activating your metaphysical abilities, it assists out-of-body journeying. Opening a new vision, this stone transports you to a quiet space of inner contemplation and soul knowing.

Between the Hills: Medjugorje

Despite conflict with the Communist authorities, people continued to witness Gospa at Medjugorje almost daily as she called for confession, reconciliation with God, prayer, and fasting. Gospa announced that she had another name, the Queen of Peace, and promised to reveal ten secrets to each of the original six visionaries. Several hundred people claimed to have seen the Sun spin on its axis and the word *peace* appear in the sky. Messages from her are still put out nearly every day on dedicated websites.

Medjugorje has become Europe's third most important Marian site with more than a million visitors each year. It is said that the footsteps of pilgrims climbing Apparition Hill have worn a rosary into the hillside.

This message via Mirjana Soldo on August 2, 2011, is typical.

> *"Dear Children, today I call you to be born anew in prayer and through the Holy Spirit, to become a new people with my Son; a people who know that if they have lost God, they have lost themselves; a people who know that, with God, despite all sufferings and trials, they are secure and saved. I call you to gather into God's family and to be strengthened with the Father's strength. As individuals, my children, you cannot stop the evil that wants to begin to rule in this world and to destroy it. But, according to God's will, all together, with my Son, you can change everything and heal the world. Thank you."*

Apparitions such as this often happen at powerful Earth-energy nodal points. Reportedly, Medjugorje lies on such a spot, which is focused through Apparition Hill rather than the village church.

Metamorphosis: Blue Quartz

A stone of peace, Blue Quartz placed over your throat chakra helps you communicate and reach out to others. By calming the mind, it assuages fear. Blue Quartz transports you through high vibrations to offer an overview of your previous lives, giving insight into your soul's plan for the present life.

BLUE QUARTZ'S PROPERTIES

If you've suffered pain in the past and are focused on revenge, if you fear being hurt, or are caught in other destructive patterns, Blue Quartz helps you forgive yourself and others. It lets you release and speak about blocked feelings. It offers comfort and insight into the consequences of grief and loss, teaching that nobody mourns alone and that, although the body dies, love does not. Blue Quartz helps you access spirit guides and higher beings. It also teaches that death occurs at the right time for the soul, no matter how inopportune it may appear.

Blue Quartz

With a pure energy that brings about cosmic alignment and attunes you to the bliss of the infinity of being, Blue Quartz with Lazulite stimulates recognition of your own divine being. Blue Quartz with Boulangerite's gentle energy brings joy to the heart and an innate sense of well-being. All Blue Quartz pushes you toward what you might be, at a pace you can accept.

BLUE QUARTZ'S HEALING POWER

Supporting the throat, immune system, spleen, endocrine system, and organs in the upper body, Blue Quartz assists detoxification and depression. It calms overstimulation and releases congestion. Indicolite Quartz is beneficial for cellular memory and overcoming insomnia and night sweats.

CONNECTING WITH BLUE QUARTZ

Blue Quartz resonates with the peace and compassion called for by the Marian messages. It takes you into a space of inner quiet to explore your spiritual nature and connect to the divine feminine.

A statue of the Virgin Mary in front of the main church at Medjugorje.

The Peace Prayer

This prayer is a variation on the Prayer of Saint Francis. It is applicable no matter what religious or spiritual orientation you follow and can be addressed to whomsoever you wish. It can be said anywhere and takes less than a minute.

PREPARATION

Cleanse your crystal and, if possible, find a quiet place to be alone. If not, simply say the prayer silently while discreetly holding your stone.

THE PRAYER

Hold your stone over your heart and repeat quietly to yourself:

"Lord, make me an instrument of your peace
Where there is hatred,
Let me sow love;
Where there is injury, pardon;
Where there is error, truth;
Where there is doubt, faith;
Where there is despair, hope;
Where there is darkness, light;
And where there is sadness, joy.
Let peace remain in my heart and
throughout the world."

Alternative Crystals

Most blue stones have peaceful, nurturing energy that connects you to the Blessed Virgin or any other manifestation of the divine feminine.

Blue Lace Agate

Chapter 15

THE UNITY OF UNIVERSE, GOD, AND HUMANITY

— HAJJI BEKTASH DERVISH TEKKE —

"For those who have Awareness, a hint is quite enough.
For the multitudes of heedless mere knowledge is useless."

—Hajji Bektash Veli, Bektashi Order of Dervishes founder and mystic

SACRED SITE
HAJJI BEKTASH DERVISH
TEKKE, HACIBEKTAS,
NORTHERN CAPPADOCIA,
TURKEY, 38°57' N 34°34' E

CORRESPONDING CRYSTAL
DIASPORE (ZULTANITE)

*T*he Hajji Bektash Tekke is an oasis of peace and quiet spiritual intensity until August, when tens of thousands of followers descend on the town. Closed by Attaturk early in the twentieth century, the thirteenth-century dervish lodge at Hacibektas reopened as a "museum" in 1964. At the far end of the outer courtyard the Üçler Fountain symbolizes Allah, Muhammad, and *Ali*, a fundamental concept of Alevi faith. Through a second courtyard, a gateway leads to where the tomb of the founder, Hajji Bektash Veli, stands amid the graves of dervishes belonging to the lodge with a venerable wishing tree in front.

✳ Northern, Cappadocia, Turkey

What this site offers you

- Profound spiritual connection
- Deep peace
- A rich inner life
- Metaphysical stimulation

Crystal Connections

No specific geology makes Hacibektas unique, except for three boulders of unknown origin near the tekke. But the site is close to the amazing sculpted stone pillars of Cappadocia, in which many stone churches are carved. From personal observation, Tektite appears to have been incorporated into the burial place of the founder, Hajji Bektash Veli. However, Turkey is unique in producing gem-quality Diaspore sold as Zultanite.

HAJJI BEKTASH TEKKE

Before entering the mausoleum, visitors see the cylindrical marble stone that belief says shows your heart is clean and your intentions pure if you can embrace it with two arms. Inside the hall, where the dervishes performed the ceremonial dance known as the kırklar semahı, twelve-sided stones called teslim tasi are exhibited. Dervishes hung these around their necks

Inside the tomb of the Bektas founder

The Üçler Fountain

as symbols of the Bektashi order. The octagonal ceiling, based on the sacred geometry of rotated squares, symbolizes the nine levels of Sufic creation. Sufism, the mystical dimension of Islam, incorporates much older metaphysical understanding.

HAJJI BEKTASH VELI

Hajji Bektash Veli was a mystic and writer, and a contemporary of the Sufi poet Mevlana Celaleddin-i Rumi. Both men were known for their piety, tolerance, and humanitarianism. Rumi wrote in Persian for the educated classes, but Hajji Bektash taught in Arabic to the peasants and Janissaries of the Sultan's army. Hajji Bektash united the Christian residents of Anatolia (then under Mongol domination) and the Muslim Turcoman immigrants, and played an important role in the formation of cultural unity and central authority in Anatolia.

Hajji Bektash Veli was born in Nishabur, Khorasan, in 1248 and spent his childhood in Khorasan. Trained in philosophy and social and positive sciences at Hodja Ahmet Yesevi's school, he traveled throughout Iran, Iraq, and Arabia. He settled in Sulucukarahoyuk (now Hacibektas) between 1275 and 1280 and founded his tekke (a Sufi place of devotion and teaching).

Hajji Bektashi taught, "Whatever you're searching for, search in yourself, it's neither in Jerusalem, Mecca nor in the Hadj." Seeking to establish the unity of "Universe, God, and Man" based on human love, he taught that all religions ultimately had the same God. In his view, humans possessed divine qualities. The first step was to know and love yourself, because "man harbors divine qualities within himself, and the man who loves himself also loves God." According to Bektashi,

> "Students hew stone,
> They hew and present it to their master,
> In every inch of the stone,
> They call God to mind."

Deeply influenced by the perfection, harmony, and order that he observed in the universe, Bektashi's basic tenets—many of which were revolutionary at the time—included equality and education for women, control of "tongue, hands, and loins" (thoughts, actions, and desires), integrity and nonjudgmentalism, not hurting anyone even though you've been hurt, and not asking anyone to do anything that would be difficult for you to do. Emphasizing the inner life, he stated, "the greatest book to read is man himself" and "the beauty of the face consists of the words you speak."

Diaspore

The Dreaming Stone: Diaspore (Zultanite)

Diaspore is found in Turkey in a rare gem quality that assists consciousness expansion. Useful for grounding high-vibration energy into the Earth, Diaspore opens the crown and higher crown chakras. Placed over the third eye, the stone promotes lucid dreaming, enhances psychic skills, and facilitates metaphysical abilities of all kinds.

DIASPORE'S PROPERTIES

A dichrotic stone, meaning its color varies when looked at from different angles, Diaspore helps you see things from different perspectives. It shows the unity of all things.

DIASPORE'S HEALING POWER

Manganese, a constituent of Diaspore, is required by the body for metabolic function, correct bone development, tissue repair, and assimilation of minerals. It supports the immune system and helps the body maintain the correct acid–alkaline balance, removing free radicals and pollutants. Diaspore releases water retention, aiding weight loss.

CONNECTING WITH DIASPORE

Place Diaspore on your third eye to open your metaphysical sight. It expands your consciousness to multidimensional awareness.

Alternative Crystals

Selenite and Apophyllite both assist in opening the crown chakras and connecting to divine light and love.

Selenite

Apophyllite

Pine ceiling showing the nine layers of creation.

Opening the Inner Eye

This exercise helps open your third eye, offering you inner sight (or insight) and metaphysical awareness.

PREPARATION

Purify your stone and ensure that you will not be disturbed. Respectfully request permission to connect to this site.

EXERCISE

Place your Diaspore over your third eye and, with half-closed eyes, gaze at the illustration of the pine ceiling. Rise through the levels. Feel your inner eye opening and your consciousness expanding. To enhance your intuition or promote insightful dreams, place the stone over your third eye or put it under your pillow.

Judy's Experience: A Spiritual High

When I entered the tekke in Hacibektas, I clearly felt a living spiritual presence. A few local people were there quietly chanting. It was energetically vibrant and profoundly uplifting. I felt I was floating above my body, propelled by a spiritual force. After visiting the tomb of the founder, Hajji Bektash Veli, I had to sit down and meditate beneath the stepped pine roof that took me through all the different levels of creation. I felt spiritually recharged; well-being poured through my whole body. The high lasted after I returned home and enriched my inner life.

Chapter 16

COMING HOME TO MOTHER AFRICA

— GORÉE ISLAND —

"Gorée Island certainly belongs to Africa and America but, on a large scale, it is a universal heritage.
It may become a land of meditation and contemplation where men, now aware of their history and its tragedy,
will appreciate even more justice and brotherhood."

—*Amadou Mahtar M'Bow, former UNESCO director–general*

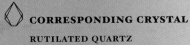 **SACRED SITE**
GORÉE ISLAND, DAKAR,
SENEGAL, 14°41' N 26°48' W

CORRESPONDING CRYSTAL
RUTILATED QUARTZ

Gorée Island, off the coast of Senegal, has become a focal point of remembrance for the millions of Africans who were enslaved in the Americas. Some 30,000 visitors a year pay their respects here. It is a place of pilgrimage for those who wish to honor their ancestry, especially those who will never know their origins.

Gorée Island

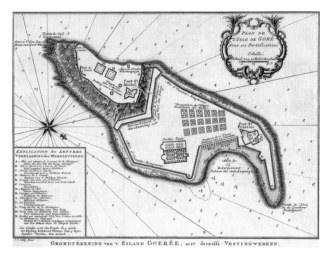

Gorée Island, Senegal

What this site offers you

- Answering the call of ancestral spirits
- Honoring African heritage
- Remembering things past
- Healing the ancestral line
- Liberation from enslavement

Crystal Connections

Rutilated Quartz contains strands of rutile, otherwise known as titanium, the mineral that colors the land of West Africa red. Years ago, a descendant of freed slaves repatriated to Sierra Leone told me this red earth was described as "the bleeding heart of our country" in memory of those forcibly taken from their homes. Rutilated Quartz is a fitting stone for this site, although it may not necessarily be found on the island. Any crystal from your homeland, wherever that may be, can be used to reconnect.

Gorée Island: Mother Africa

For 300 years, the House of Slaves shipped Africans to the Americas under horrendous conditions. After capture in the interior of Africa, slaves were force marched to the coast, weighed and priced, then sold and branded. It could take months before slaves were shipped. Meanwhile they waited, chained in dungeons. Food was deliberately restricted so slaves would fight among themselves rather than banding against their captors. Slaves who died were thrown out of the "Doorway of No Return" into the sea. Estimates vary widely; some authorities suggest as many as 5 million died, others say far fewer.

But slavery is much older than this. Slaves were taken from many other places in the past and slavery continues to this day. This site acts as a focal point for every person or culture that has been enslaved. Guided tours of the dungeons on Gorée ensure that the awful history of slavery will never be forgotten.

Modern-day visitors perform ceremonies here to celebrate "coming home to Mother Africa." They invoke their ancestors and pray for them, lighting candles and making offerings of flowers. Plaques have been placed at the site, and the home of Anne-Marie Javouhey, a nineteenth-century nun who campaigned to end slavery, is maintained as an antislavery memorial.

Rutilated Quartz

The Power of Purification: Rutilated Quartz

Often known as Angel's Hair because of the fine strands of rutile, Rutilated Quartz is a powerful, purifying Quartz. This stone connects to the highest angelic frequencies and contains the perfect balance of cosmic light and creative power. It opens portals and high-dimensional possibilities.

RUTILATED QUARTZ'S PROPERTIES
Spiritual evolution is accelerated by Rutilated Quartz, which opens interdimensional metaphysical sight. It amplifies the power of thought, so that what you think manifests in the outer world. If the power is misused selfishly or abusively, it backfires, but it can dramatically transform your world for the good of all. An efficient purifier of toxic thoughts and constrictive emotions, Rutilated Quartz liberates you from the past, dissolving barriers to spiritual evolution so your soul purpose comes into play.

Useful in past-life or ancestral healing, it promotes insight into the core issue and encourages forgiveness and release. It reveals dis-ease or karmic patterns that have deliberately been assumed for soul learning. At an emotional level, Rutilated Quartz heals the past and dissolves the deeper causes of depression, phobias, or anxiety. It is an efficient Earth healer.

RUTILATED QUARTZ'S HEALING POWER

By drawing off negative energy and infusing new vitality, Rutilated Quartz provides a firm foundation for new energetic patterns to be imprinted into cells. Crystal workers use it to balance the thyroid, heal the lungs, and stimulate cellular growth. Placed on the solar plexus or thymus, it treats chronic dis-eases and sexual dysfunction.

CONNECTING WITH RUTILATED QUARTZ

This connection offers you a potent source of energy and profound healing for the past. It takes you journeying down your ancestral line to give healing to all who have carried pain or anguish. It helps reprogram your DNA, clearing inherited patterns so you move forward, freed from the past.

Coming Home

This meditation helps you return to your roots and heals your ancestral line. It offers you liberation and emancipation from anything that holds you captive, setting you free to be your true self. It also helps you put down roots in a country that you have made your home. The journey lets you step through the doorway into true freedom—knowledge of who you are—and strengthens your spiritual roots.

PREPARATION

If you have photographs of your ancestors or your place of origin, position them in front of you. Light a candle and lay out flowers. Purify your stone and ensure that you will not be disturbed. Respectfully request permission to connect to this site.

The Doorway of No Return, House of Slaves.

THE JOURNEY HOME

Holding your Rutilated Quartz, half-close your eyes and look at the doorway. Honor those who have walked this way before you, their struggles and their pain. Let the light of the Quartz go to them to heal that pain, lifting them and helping them pass on to higher dimensions and new possibilities. Send them on their way with dignity, unconditional love, and forgiveness in their hearts.

Taking your courage in both hands, picture yourself walking through this doorway so that you fly free, leaving behind any bondage or restriction, angst or anguish you may have been feeling. Feel yourself moving into liberation and emancipation, into your birthright of full humanity and expanded consciousness. Travel where your Rutilated Quartz takes you, or simply sit quietly absorbing the energy.

When you are ready to return, set the Quartz on the photographs of your ancestors or ancestral home and leave them in a place where you will see them often. Blow out the candle, sending your ancestral memories on their way with love.

Picture a bubble of protection around you. Connect to the Earth beneath your feet. Feel roots growing from the soles of each foot, passing down into the ground and twining together at the Earth star chakra. These roots extend deep into the center of the Earth, hooking around the iron ball at its core. They hold you lightly in incarnation and anchor you to the place you have chosen to call home.

Alternative Crystals

Any African crystals, such as Rose Quartz, Brandenberg Amethyst, Ajoite, Malachite, or Spirit Quartz, are suitable for this meditation. Or, choose a crystal from your homeland.

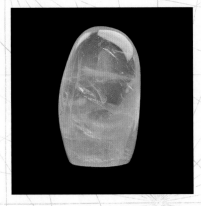

Rose Quartz

Brandenberg Amethyst

Ajoite

Malachite

Spirit Quartz

Chapter 17

A METAPHYSICAL LANDSCAPE

— THE GREAT PYRAMID —

"Did you not know O Asclepius that Egypt is an image of Heaven, or, to speak more exactly, that in Egypt all the operations of the powers which rule and work in Heaven have been transferred to the Earth below? Nay, it should rather be said that the whole cosmos dwells in this our land as in its sanctuary."

—Hermes Trismegistus, ancient Egyptian sage

SACRED SITE

THE GREAT PYRAMID, GIZA PLATEAU, CAIRO, EGYPT, 29°59' N 31°09' E

CORRESPONDING CRYSTAL

ASWAN GRANITE

*T*he Great Pyramid is the last of the Seven Wonders of the Ancient World. Built to face true north, it has stood for at least five thousand years. Its outer casing is limestone, but gallery linings and the sarcophagus at the pyramid's heart are Pink Aswan Granite. Said by Egyptologists to be a burial chamber, the pyramid is a "stargate": a giant energy amplifier, a solar-powered resurrection machine, or an acoustically driven, psychoactive temple of initiation depending on your point of view.

Crystal Connections

Aswan Granite helps you make a profound connection to ancient Egypt and the magical knowledge of that time. It transports you into a world where spiritual transformation is not only possible, it is the raison d'être. The ancient Egyptians' preoccupation with death arose because they believed the soul lived on in other dimensions of reality. With this stone, you journey to the stars and beyond.

STONES IN THE GREAT PYRAMID

The stones used for the Great Pyramid came from several sources—the bulk from Limestone quarries on the Giza Plateau itself, white Limestone for the outer casing stones from Tura (a short distance upriver), and Pink Granite from Aswan some 423 miles (681 km) away. The sarcophagus at its heart was hewn out of a single block of Pink Granite. Graywacke, a coarse-grained gray Sandstone, was also used and a black Basalt pavement surrounds the pyramid's temple. In one of the passages sits a three-stone plug of a rare Red Granite identical to that of the mountain on which Moses is said to have received the Ten Commandments. Moses, of course, lived long after the pyramid's construction, but this may be an example of stone being brought from one already sacred site to another, for the sanctity of that mountain predated Moses by several thousand years.

In its heyday, the pyramid would have been a gleaming black-and-white mountain sitting on a dusty, yellow-brown plateau alongside a shining ribbon of water. The dazzling structure could be seen from the mountains of Israel.

The Great Pyramid

The throat chakra of the world, the Great Pyramid is the most enduring symbol of ancient Egypt and one of the most enigmatic. It stands on a nodal crossing point of powerful Earth energy lines, which create a vortex. Although archaeologists say it is the tomb of Pharaoh Khufu, no trace of burial has been found except the empty, sarcophagus at its center. Metaphysicians believe

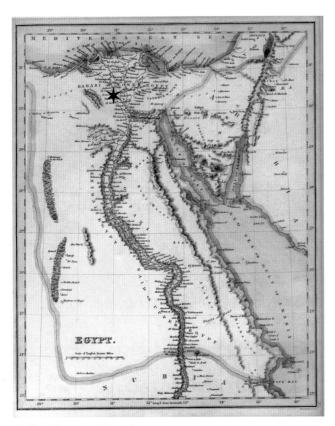

★ Giza Plateau, Cairo, Egypt

What this site offers you

- Expanded consciousness
- A sense of your greater self
- An opportunity to tap into cosmological energy
- Reconnection to temple lives and ancient Egyptian knowledge
- An understanding of ancient vibrational technology

The Giza Pyramid complex

it was an initiation chamber and a portal to celestial realms. As one Egyptologist said, "the pyramid does not stand for anything visible, it makes something visible."

That "something" is a precise relationship between the stone structure and the heavens. The pyramid is accurately aligned to the cardinal points of the compass and to parts of the sky that are home to fixed stars and the eternally rotating zodiac. This is the place of "here and not-here, now and not-now," a dimension where heavenly time reigns.

"To build a sacred space was to establish not only a spatial but also a temporal link to the heavens, it was a realization of eternity," writes Jan Assmann in *The Mind of Egypt*. "Monumental time is heavenly time."

A pyramid signifies a sacred space that embodies celestial correspondence. All Egyptian monuments display this cosmological relationship. Temples, too, were numinous spaces and, as John Anthony West puts it in *Serpent in the Sky*, "the Egyptian temple was the model of the universe seen from the point of view of the neter [god] to which it was consecrated."

MYTHOLOGY, LEGENDS, AND LORE: THROUGH THE PORTAL OF IMMORTALITY

"O King, you are this great star, the companion of Orion, who traverses the sky with Orion, who navigates the Duat with Osiris; you ascend from the East of the sky, being renewed at your due season."

Pyramid Texts Utterance 466

From the pyramid, Pharaoh journeyed to the stars, spoke to the gods, and performed the rituals that kept Egypt safe and eternal. The pyramid had a separate pyramidion or ben-ben at its tip. Esoteric lore says it was made of Quartz, a powerful generator and transmitter of energy. Archaeological evidence suggests it may have been black Granite, also a generator of energy, providing a striking contrast to the polished white Limestone sides.

Inventor and engineer Sir William Siemens reported that, standing on top of the Great Pyramid, his Arab guide called attention to the fact that, when he held up his hand, a ringing noise could be heard. Siemens raised his index finger and felt a distinct prickling. Drinking from a wine bottle he had brought along, he received a slight electric shock. Wrapping damp newspaper around the bottle, Siemens held it above his head and it filled with electricity. When sparks began issuing from the top, the Arab guides accused him of witchcraft. One who tried to seize the bottle was knocked senseless. Such experiences have led to the idea that the pyramid is a gigantic energy-generating machine.

When Napoleon spent the night in the sarcophagus in the King's Chamber in 1798, he reportedly emerged white and visibly shaken. When asked what had occurred he replied, "If I told you, you would never believe me." He took the secret to his grave.

ARCHAEOASTRONOMY

"As truly as your monument stands on its foundations
Like heaven on its pillars . . .
Its years are those of akhet [the horizon],
Its months are those of the decan [fixed] stars.
It knows no destruction on earth for all eternity."

Egyptologist Jan Assmann, citing Montet's
Le rituel de la fondation des temples egyptiens

Orthodox Egyptologists suggest that the somewhat off-center, random alignment of the three main Giza pyramids is the result of the terrain. Archaeoastronomers propose that the pyramids are part of a star map, mirroring the stars in Orion's belt, and that the Nile follows the same course on the ground as the Milky Way does in the sky. Each reflects the other: a cosmological correspondence. Shafts and alignments in the pyramid have been shown to point to fixed stars, as does the grand staircase, and to the rising of certain zodiacal constellations at specific times in the sidereal year. (Due to precession of the equinoxes, these signs no longer align but would once have held profound significance.)

Unorthodox Egyptologists go further and state that the whole of Egypt was a map of the heavens laid out on the ground—above and below were one. The map was designed to help Pharaoh navigate his way through the Duat, the nighttime journey taken by the solar boat. It was also the guide for his shamanic journey to the stars in search of renewal and resurrection. The Great Pyramid also acts as a solar calendar whose shadows mark the equinoxes and solstices.

LIVING GEOMETRY: SQUARING THE CIRCLE

"Geometry is knowledge that appears to be produced by human beings, yet whose meaning is totally independent of them."

Rudolf Steiner, philosopher, mystic, and metaphysician

The Great Pyramid has been described as a repository of universal mathematical standards. It stands at the exact center of the Earth's greatest land mass. Its north–south axis (31° E) is the longest land meridian, and the east–west axis (30° N) is the longest parallel crossing land. These axes cross at Giza. The pyramid lies in the center of gravity of the land area of the planet, dividing the Earth's land mass into virtually equal quarters.

The platform on which it stands was cut from the bedrock with an accuracy of ½ inch (1.3 cm). The sides of the pyramid are slightly concave—an effect discovered in 1940 from aerial photographs. The radius of the bow is equal to the radius of the Earth. Measured with modern laser instruments, these precisely cut stones replicate exactly the curvature of the Earth.

The pyramids were built in sacred cubits. There are 25 pyramid inches in a cubit. Measured from corner to corner, the distance across the Great Pyramid is 365.24 cubits, the number of days in a solar year. If the circumference of the pyramid is divided by twice its height the result is 3.14159, or pi.

Modern mathematicians find it difficult to believe that the geometry of the Great Pyramid was based on the golden ratio and pi hundreds of years before fundamental geometric principles were "discovered" by Greek mathematicians. But the pyramid clearly incorporates sacred geometry into its structure. The corners are virtually perfect right angles and its sides slope at an angle of 51°52', reflecting the latitude at which on the equinoxes day and night are of equal length and the Sun sets due west. Through a complex mathematical formula, if the base length of the Great Pyramid is equated with the diameter of the Earth, the radius of the Moon can be found by subtracting the radius of the Earth from the height of the pyramid (www.world-mysteries.com).

THE SOUND OF ALL THINGS

"The Great Pyramid is designed to be operated by nothing more than a vibrational and electromagnetic field created by a human being."

www.soundofallthings.com

As befits the throat chakra of the world, the Great Pyramid is rich in ancient sound technology. Esoteric tradition states that sound was used to maneuver the enormous blocks into place, and the entire structure with its chambers, galleries, and shafts is an acoustically resonant chamber.

People who tone or chant within the pyramid report extraordinary experiences and life-changing events. The whole body resonates in sympathy with the vibrational field and harmonic overlays created by the human voice, amplified by the paramagnetic resonance of the pyramid's Granite-lined walls and soundboards. The builders were likely aware of the profound effect of acoustic technology, utilizing it for healing, consciousness expansion, and spiritual transformation. The sarcophagus at the pyramid's heart has inspired many visionary and levitation experiences, especially when activated by sound.

Aswan Granite

Aswan Granite: Stone of the Gods

Aswan Granite incorporates glittering Quartz, Pyrite, and Feldspar crystals within its structure, giving it a crystalline appearance that takes a high polish. It had a particularly strong connection to the heavens and channeled the power of the Sun god to Earth.

ASWAN GRANITE'S PROPERTIES

Aswan Granite has the highest paramagnetic resonance of all Granites and is piezoelectric, creating a powerful current that flows with a measurable field. The stone has a profound bioenergetic effect on the human body. Amplifying sound waves, it creates harmonic overtones when the rock is struck or activated by a human voice. High in Qi, sound rocks convey vibrational healing to the human body. Granite is an excellent gridding stone for creating a sacred space in which to perform magical and transformational rituals. Aswan Granite facilitates reconnection to temple lives and arcane knowledge.

◄ Granite soundboards in the Grand Gallery.

ASWAN GRANITE'S HEALING POWER

Granite has a stabilizing effect on the human energy field. It realigns the subtle bodies with the physical, stimulating electrical activity in cells, and activates the immune response. Neutralizing the ill effects of toxic Earth energy lines, it reenergizes the Earth's magnetic grid. Granite has long been credited with the ability to heal rickets, rheumatism, and infertility.

The Pyramid Journey

This journey takes you into the heart of the Great Pyramid to lie in the sarcophagus of initiation. From there, you journey to the stars and beyond. It helps you to know the fullness of your own soul and the multidimensions beyond our three-dimensional reality.

PREPARATION

Ensure that you will not be disturbed for half an hour. Respectfully request permission to connect to this site. Sit or lie flat, preferably wrapped in a blanket. Appropriate music, such as Steven Halpern's "Initiation" (recorded within the Great Pyramid), assists your journey. Set a timer so you will be called to return after thirty minutes.

JOURNEY OF INITIATION

Hold your stone between your hands. Close your eyes and breathe gently, focusing on your breath. With each exhalation, release any tension you may be feeling. With each inhalation, draw in peace and quietude. When you are ready, focus your attention on your third eye, above and between your eyebrows.

Picture yourself standing in the sand on the banks of the Nile in front of the Great Pyramid. An avenue of gleaming Limestone leads straight to the pyramid's entrance. As you walk up the pathway, you see the guardian of the pyramid waiting to greet you. He leads you through the enormous doorway and points along the gallery lit by flickering torches. The way is narrow, twisting and turning until at last you come to the staircase rising before you. As you mount these steps, you hear sound resonating around you; the acoustic chamber has been activated.

The Sarcophagus with a guardian in the background

Before you is the huge granite sarcophagus. The guardian leads you to it and helps you settle yourself inside. He taps the sarcophagus with his staff. As he leaves the chamber he extinguishes the torches.

A beam of starlight falls from a shaft above you. The sarcophagus vibrates, shaking loose your etheric body. You feel your etheric body being drawn up and out of the shaft. Transport awaits you.

When it is time to return, the guardian lights the torches again. He touches you with his staff to reunite your physical and etheric bodies, and helps you out of the sarcophagus. He leads the way out of the pyramid.

As you step out of the pyramid, wrap a cloak of protection around yourself and greet the rising Sun. You are reborn. When the meditation is over, stamp your feet to connect with the Earth again.

Alternative Crystals

Any type of Granite is suitable for this journey, including Texan or Indian Pink. You could also use Quartz or Basalt.

Indian Pink Granite

Clear Quartz

Black Basalt

Andrea's Story: Celestial Connections

I saw a chariotlike vehicle, which had no horses or driver. The wheels were massive and they were spinning really fast and coming toward me. I got on and after a short while it seemed as though we had stopped, but then I saw things zooming past me and realized we were still moving very quickly. We pulled up at a beautiful galaxy and I felt such love I didn't want to move. I was dragged on reluctantly and came to a place covered in sand.

At first, I couldn't see anything, but then I saw shimmers. They became clearer and I knew they were beings of light-energy. The place was full of them. They started congregating in one place and I equated it to a chapel—it was a very sacred space. They connected together in a honeycomb shape. If one was missing, light was put there. The honeycomb grew and grew. I've since realized that this is where we download all the knowledge we have learned from our different experiences so that we can grow.

There was also a place made of different-sized pillars of crystals with points at the top. I went to the crystal pillar of my choice and entered it. I could see all the matrices of the crystal and its nooks and crannies. I could bathe in its energy and, as the Sun shone through, I was filled with the different colors. If I went to a different section I could download learning. If I needed healing this would be given. I could play games—it was a space where I could be young and free. A place where anything is possible.

When I had finished, I left, knowing the crystal would welcome me back anytime. When I was writing this, I also realized that the crystals were learning from us and they were growing with this knowledge, and that everybody would experience the right thing each time they entered.

Chapter 18

THE SANCTUARY OF SHE WHO IS POWERFUL

— SEKHMET SANCTUARY, KARNAK TEMPLE —

"The slim beam of light falling sharply from a hole in the roof illuminated her magnificent black Basalt figure. Shining out from the surrounding darkness, she was awesome. Her eyes drew me forward and I wanted to fall to my knees, to prostrate myself full length on the dirt floor, to worship her."

—*Judy Hall,* Torn Clouds

SACRED SITE
SEKHMET SANCTUARY, KARNAK TEMPLE, LUXOR, EGYPT, 25°41' N 32°39' E

CORRESPONDING CRYSTAL
BLACK BASALT

Karnak is a powerful, solar-aligned temple standing on the east bank of the Nile at Thebes in upper Egypt. Its obelisks draw the power of the Sun god to Earth. Its enormous hypostyle hall maps out the cycles and eclipses of the Moon. Beyond the main temple lies Temple Mut, which archaeologists are slowly resurrecting from the encroaching sand. More than 1,500 Basalt statues of Sekhmet have been uncovered from around Mut's sacred lake. But the main power of Sekhmet lies in a tiny, remote chapel tucked away within the confines of Karnak Temple. The sanctuary of Sekhmet is, for me, one of the most powerful places on the planet. I simply had to include her sanctuary here.

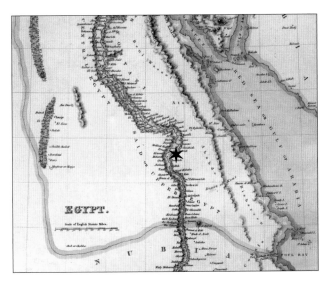

★ The Upper Nile

What this site offers you

- The opportunity to stand fully in your power
- The awe-filled and numinous power of the divine

Crystal Connections

Massive statues of Sekhmet were almost always created from Granite or Basalt, although smaller ones are made of Aventurine, Carnelian, Calcite, or Lapis Lazuli—the semiprecious gems of ancient Egypt.

The Sekhem Sekhmet Temple

To reach this sanctuary, you first must pass through that of her husband, the creator God Ptah. His tiny statue is of a potter tending his wheel, creating human-kind—hardly a fitting preparation for the awesome sight of his towering, 8-foot (2.4 m)-tall lion-headed wife striding toward you out of the gloom. In her hands she holds the rod of power and the ankh, symbol of eternal life. At noon an opening in the temple roof channels sunlight down onto the crown of the statue's head, firing her essence.

MYTHOLOGY, LEGENDS, AND LORE

In a folk memory of an ancient ritual, the temple guardians delight in performing "the blessing of Sekhmet," touching your hands first to the Lady's chakras and then to your own. In sensitive individuals, the ritual can cause a spontaneous rise of kundalini power up the spine, an echo of the cosmic orgasm celebrated in her ancient rituals.

Sekhmet's name derives from the ancient Egyptian word *sekhem*, meaning "power." One of the oldest Egyptian deities and daughter of the Sun god Ra, she is usually portrayed as a lion-headed woman with a Sun disk on her head. She was the patron of physicians, and priestesses of Sekhmet were skilled healers and midwives. This goddess possessed the power to bring disease or health. Associated with the searing heat of the midday Sun, she was the "Lady of the Flame." Above all, she was the protector of Ma'at, balance or justice.

Sekhmet was also the "Lady of Terror" who inflicted great suffering on those who displeased her. According to myth, her father, Ra, grew tired of the machinations of humans and sent Sekhmet to destroy humankind in an orgy of bloodletting. She was stopped by a cunningly disguised lake of wine, which the goddess mistook for blood. On her recovery, she became a goddess of healing but retained her awesome power.

Gateway to the sanctuary of Sekhmet

Black Basalt

Black Basalt: Stabilizing the Universe

Basalt is a powerfully magnetic rock spewed from ancient volcanoes. In ancient Egypt, it was used to house the energies of the gods, stabilizing the universe by their presence. Providing solid support during life changes, it assists transformation.

BASALT'S PROPERTIES

Making you more resilient when under pressure, Basalt helps you move fluidly through changes in your life circumstances while remaining centered. If you need an anchor, it connects your physical body to the Earth and your soul into your body. By helping you maintain emotional detachment, it provides support as you explore the darker corners of your inner self. The stone lets you realize that life's traumas and dramas ultimately polish the soul.

Basalt helps transmute anger and resentment. This stone is an excellent destressor, encouraging relaxation and helping to realign meridians. Hold Black Basalt over your solar plexus for stability or anger release. Grid it in areas of environmental instability to stabilize the Earth.

BASALT'S HEALING POWER

Basalt releases tension from the body at a deep level, assisting muscles and imbuing strength and cohesion. Basalt also optimizes your energy levels. Activating the intestines, it encourages detoxification. The ancients used it to ensure fertility of the body and the land.

Alternative Stone

Granite has similar stabilizing properties.

Granite (gray)

Sekhmet: She Who Is Powerful

The Blessing Ritual

This ritual takes you to meet the Goddess Sekhmet to connect to sekhem power.

PREPARATION

Ensure that you will not be disturbed for ten minutes. Respectfully request permission to connect to this site.

THE BLESSING OF SEKHMET

Standing quietly with your eyes closed, focus your attention on the stone in your hands. Picture yourself standing in front of Sekhmet as the sunlight from the roof lights up her awesome face.

While uttering the ancient invocation *sa sekhem sahu*, place the stone to your base (root) chakra over the pubic bone and invite the power of the goddess to enter. Slowly move the stone up to the sacral chakra below your navel; pause and allow the power to enter. Move

the stone to the solar plexus chakra, then to the heart, the throat, the third eye, and finally, your crown. As you hold the stone above your head, feel a beam of light illuminating your crown chakra and connecting you to the awesome power of the divine feminine that passes down your spine to settle into the dantien just below your navel where that power is stored until needed. Bring the stone back to your base chakra. Say aloud: "I stand in my power."

Thank the goddess and disconnect from the stone. Picture a bubble of protection all around you. Whenever you need power, pick up the stone and hold it just below your navel to release the energy.

Megan's Experience: Touched by She Who Is Powerful

A gate opened and I was pushed into a dark place. Panic rose in my chest, my heart leapt and surged, I could not breathe. Air, I must have air. Helplessly, my arms flailed and my outstretched fingers touched warm stone.

"Moment. Moment . . ."

The scuttling and rattling sounds did nothing to reassure me. Suddenly sunlight reflecting from a flattened tin can dazzled my eyes. On a plinth, a tiny statue sat before a chipped and battered potter's wheel. The great creator had been reduced to this? If only I had an offering to make. Why? What hold did he have on me? How did I know who this anonymous being was anyway? My head spun stars to fill the smoke-blackened ceiling above me. Robed women moved like wraiths around a cooking fire, tending small children. How could anyone have moved in here, lived in this god-haunted place? Perhaps they thought their Christian symbols would protect them. Was I going mad?

Suddenly, a stream of camera-bedecked Japanese tourists issued from a recessed doorway and disappeared into dust.

Dumbstruck, I awaited my fate. A heavy door was unchained, revealing only blackness. Taut with terror, I was unable to move. The door swung back.

"Come, come." They gestured me forward. "The blessing of Sekhmet."

Dimly, I made out a tall, majestic form.

The door closed and a shaft of sunlight pierced the gloom. It illuminated a face I knew well—it had haunted my dreams and drawn me here to her temple. The proud, leonine head sat atop a sensuous woman's body, her breasts bared. The face was powerful like a lion's, compassionate like a woman's. The slim beam of light falling sharply from a hole in the roof illuminated her magnificent Black Basalt figure. Shining out from the surrounding darkness, she was awesome. She must have been 8-feet [2.4 m] tall. Her eyes drew me forward and I wanted to fall to my knees, to prostrate myself full length on the dirt floor, to worship her, but the guardian took my hand and pulled me up.

I felt myself slipping, sliding away. Falling into nothingness . . .

(The remainder of this experience, based on my own, with its graphic reliving of the Sekhmet myth is in my novel *Torn Clouds*.)

Chapter 19

SPEAKING WITH GOD

— MOUNT SINAI —

"There are a few places in the world where you are confronted with such a mountainscape as that of the Sinai. The landscape is both visually overpowering and at peace — as if nature in enacting its script has become frozen in stone."

—Center for Sinai

SACRED SITE
MOUNT SINAI, MOUNT SINAI PENINSULA, EGYPT 28°32' N 33°58' E

CORRESPONDING CRYSTAL
SMOKY QUARTZ

Mount Sinai is revered by the Jewish, Christian, and Islamic faiths as the site where God spoke to the prophet Moses. Tradition has it that Sinai is where Moses saw the burning bush and received instructions for making the crystal-studded Breastplate of the High Priest. Connecting to this site plugs you directly into the heart of God.

Crystal Connections

Rising out of the arid Sinai Desert, Mount Sinai is a comparatively young Granite mountain thrust up through a sea of thousand-million-year-old rock by volcanic activity and tectonic plate movement. It contains both primal igneous and transformed metamorphic rocks. Such rocks symbolize humanity's spiritual yearnings and encourage personal growth. Metamorphic rocks help you find survival strategies and ways to cope with constant stress—very necessary for a tribe that had been wandering in the wilderness. Fissures within the mountain's rock are studded with Smoky Quartz and Chalcedony deposits, forming its bones. Turquoise, manganese, and copper are also found in Sinai.

Mount Sinai: The Mountain of God

Mount Sinai has been sacred for over four millennia. When Moses first set foot upon it, God told him to remove his shoes because he stood on holy ground. There is debate as to whether this is Moses's mountain, as archaeology points to other possibilities. The tradition seems to have been started by Christian hermits living in caves at its base in the third century CE, but Jews and Muslims also accept it as the Old Testament site. Thousands of pilgrims flock to its summit. Beneath the 7,113-foot (2,168 m) summit lies the Plain of ar-Raaha, where the Israelites reputedly camped while Moses ascended the mountain before erecting the tabernacle to shelter the Ark of the Covenant. Saint Catherine's Monastery sits at Sinai's foot and two tiny chapels are on the summit, one a mosque, the other Greek Orthodox.

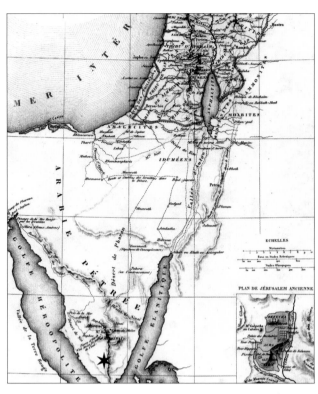

✴ Mount Sinai, Egypt

What this site offers you

- Puts you in touch with the divine
- Opens your intuition and lets you hear your inner voice
- Takes you to the root of Judeo–Christian and Islamic traditions
- Makes you aware of being an integral part of the human family on Earth
- Connects you to All That Is and the huge cycles of historical time

Moses on Mount Sinai: artist's impression

When Moses came down again, it was with instructions to make the Breastplate of the High Priest, a crystal-studded pouch with twelve crystals, one for each of the twelve tribes of Israel.

THE BREASTPLATE OF THE HIGH PRIEST

Possibly the most significant ancient crystal artifact is the Breastplate of the High Priest. The "breastplate" probably didn't look anything like the representations we find today as the Hebrew word means "pouch." Aaron could have been wearing a woven linen bag around his neck and chest, with twelve engraved crystals attached.

It is impossible to know exactly which stones were used as each biblical translation specifies a different list. Exodus, chapter 25 continues:

> *"And thou shall make the breastplate of judgement with cunning work; after the work of the ephod thou shalt make it; of gold, of blue, and of purple, and of scarlet, and of fine linen shalt thou make it . . . And thou shalt set in it settings of stones, even four rows of stones: the first row shall be a sardius [Sardonyx], a topaz [possibly Smoky Quartz], and a carbuncle [a term used for Garnet and Carnelian]: this shall be the first row. And the second row shall be an emerald [possibly Green Aventurine], a sapphire [probably Lapis Lazuli], and a diamond [probably clear Quartz] . . . And the third row a ligure [translation unknown], an agate, and an amethyst. And the fourth row a beryl, and an onyx, and a jasper; they shall be set in gold in their enclosings . . . And thou shalt put in the breastplate of judgement the U-rim and the Thum-mim."*

Given the presence of Turquoise and Smoky Quartz in the vicinity and their popularity in Egypt (from where the Israelites had traveled), it would be surprising if these stones did not form part of the Breastplate. Diamonds, Sapphires, and gem-quality Emeralds were virtually unknown in that area at the time, but clear Quartz, Lapis, and Aventurine were available. The pouch also contained the Urim and Thummin. No one is certain precisely what these were, possibly meteorites or precious stones.

"Steps of penitence"—3,750 of them—lead to the mountain's summit, although there is an easier path. Most pilgrims climb in the dark to avoid the heat of the day and to watch the Sun rise over the desert. On the peak of Mount Sinai, Holy Trinity church stands over the rock from which the tablets of the law were made. In the western wall of the chapel is a cleft in the rock where Moses sheltered from God's glory (Exodus 33:22).

MYTHOLOGY, LEGENDS, AND LORE

The Old Testament gives a vivid account of the meeting of Moses with his God:

> *" And it came to pass on the third day in the morning, that there were thunders and lightnings, and a thick cloud upon the mount, and the voice of the trumpet exeeding loud . . . And mount Sinai was altogether on a smoke because the Lord descended upon it in fire, and the smoke thereof ascended as the smoke of a furnace and the whole mount quaked greatly . . . The glory of the Lord abode upon mount Sinai, and the cloud covered it six days; and the seventh day God called unto Moses out of the midst of the cloud. And the appearance of the glory of the Lord was like devouring fire on the top of the mount in the eyes of the children of Israel. And Moses entered into the midst of the cloud, and went up into the mount; and Moses was in the mount forty days and forty nights."*

> *Exodus, chapter 25,* King James Authorized Bible

St. Catherine's Monastery lies at the foot of Mt. Sinai.

The historian Josephus gives us an apocryphal account of the use of the Urim and Thummin, but as the Breastplate had been lost 500 years previously in Babylon he could not have seen it in action.

"From the stones which the High Priest wore (these were sardonyxes and I hold it superfluous to describe their nature, since it is known to all), there emanated a light, as often as God was present at the sacrifices that which was worn on the right shoulder instead of a clasp emitting a radiance sufficient to give light even to those far away, although the stone previously lacked this splendour . . . I am about to relate something still more wonderful, namely that God announced victory by means of the twelve stones worn by the High Priest on his breast."

Josephus highlights an important point. During biblical times, crystals were used to ascertain the will of God—in other words, for divination. They were strongly associated with the sacred. Later, according to Revelations, these same stones would be the foundation for the New Jerusalem.

THE MONASTERY

Saint Catherine's Monastery is one of the earliest Christian communities. It sits at the foot of an inaccessible gorge and, early in the Christian era, many pilgrims came here. Helena, a fourth-century Byzantine empress, constructed the first chapel, known as the Chapel of the Burning Bush. A rare shrub, Rubus sanctus—the original burning bush—grew there then as it does today.

Saint Catherine's Monastery and the Burning Bush.

Mount Sinai.

According to legend, angels flew the body of Saint Catherine, an early Christian martyr, to the top of Mount Sinai after her death. It was apparently found, uncorrupted, by monks some 300 years later and placed in the monastery. To protect the monks and the chapel from Bedouin marauders, a fortresslike basilica was built around the chapel in CE 542.

THE PEOPLE

Moses is the best-known biblical personage associated with Sinai. Having brought his people out of Egypt, he received the Ten Commandments here. But he isn't the only Old Testament figure associated with the site. Seven hundred and fifty steps below the summit lies Elijah's Basin, the plateau where Elijah traditionally spent forty days and nights communing with his God in a cave.

The prophet Muhammad also visited the site. Having been well received by the Christian monks, Muhammad gave his personal pledge of protection to the monastery, incumbent on all Muslims even to this day.

Purification: Smoky Quartz

Smoky Quartz is a highly effective grounding stone that transmutes negative energies. Protective during meditation, it expands consciousness and literally brings the divine down to Earth. This is an excellent stone for lifting fear and depression. It helps you trust the universe while formulating survival strategies.

SMOKY QUARTZ'S PROPERTIES

Smoky Quartz encourages you to care for the environment and makes you aware of how negative energies pollute the Earth. Extremely efficient at blocking geopathic and electromagnetic stress, the stone helps purify and realign our planet's energy meridians. It also realigns energies within the human body.

Excellent for people who become ungrounded in their search for the spiritual, Smoky Quartz anchors your energies and brings your insights into everyday reality. This strengthening stone helps you adjust to being in physical incarnation while simultaneously raising your vibrations so that you make a spiritual connection. If you suffer from melancholy or depression, it lifts your spirits and instills confidence in yourself and your future. Smoky Quartz strengthens your ability to survive and supports your faith.

SMOKY QUARTZ'S HEALING POWER

Smoky Quartz eases stress and enhances libido. A powerful detoxifier on all levels, it draws off negative energies or blocks emanations that could cause disease. It is used for pain relief and cramps in muscles, hips, abdomen, and nerve tissue. The stone energetically draws off fluid and assists the body's assimilation of minerals.

CONNECTING WITH SMOKY QUARTZ

Gazing into the depths of this crystal helps you focus your attention away from the outside world and into your inner self. It expands your awareness and takes you into a timeless space where you hear the divine speaking to you. This stone helps you know that you are part of All That Is.

Smoky Quartz

Alternative Crystals

Chalcedony geodes make an excellent focus for meditation. Alternatively, use any of the crystals in the Breastplate of the High Priest.

Chalcedony Geode

Hearing the Still, Small Voice Within

This meditation connects you to your intuition and takes you into communion with the divine.

PREPARATION

Ensure that you are in a quiet, safe place where you won't be interrupted for fifteen to thirty minutes. Sit comfortably, holding your cleansed and dedicated crystal. Respectfully request permission to connect to this site.

THE MEDITATION

Holding a purified Smoky Quartz, half-close your eyes and gaze into the crystal's depths. Breathe gently, withdrawing your attention from the outside world and focusing it on the crystal. Follow the planes and canyons in its interior until you reach the center. Let the voice of your intuition makes itself heard.

Close your eyes and feel the energy of the crystal running up your arms and into your head. In imagination, you are transported to the top of the Mountain of God. Here, you commune with the divine as it descends around you.

When you are ready to return, bring your attention back into the room. Picture a bubble of protection around you. Put down the crystal, but know that the contact with your intuition and with the divine continues.

Christine's Experience: Rising Above

I hiked up Mount Sinai to watch the sunrise. It was very cold, and the night was beautifully clear and bright with stars. As we climbed, I began to feel increasingly emotional. At one point, I thought I might burst into tears, but I couldn't understand why. The mountain loomed above me, and I could see only where my torch shone. It grew colder, and we seemed to have been climbing for a long time. The air was growing thinner, but I was determined to get to the top. I sensed that what I was feeling was connected very strongly to Mount Sinai.

We reached the top and were surprised to see many people there, wrapped up in blankets facing the east, waiting for the Sun to rise. I sat cross legged and stared across the peaks surrounding us, into the darkness. I felt even more emotional and wanted to sob. The sky began to lighten as the Sun rose. I became still, and focused on what was before me.

I began to feel as if I, too, were rising above everything. It was as if Mount Sinai was detaching itself from the Earth and floating. I saw the Earth below me moving in the golden light of the rising Sun. It was as if the Earth itself were bowing in obeisance to the Sun, as if worshipping it. I merged with whatever was happening . . . I had no boundaries. I was one with everything; there was no time. I just was, and everything just was. It was that simple. The Sun rose higher and the moment passed.

When we began our descent I felt strangely light, as if a great burden had been lifted from me. It was as if a hole had been burned through my heart chakra, and it was bright and open.

I wanted to take a reminder of the mountains home with me and bought three stones from a Bedouin, a beautiful mix of Smoky Quartz and Brown Granite. I hold one of them in my hand when I feel stressed or anxious. I find their energy calming.

My mother had died eighteen months before my trip to Egypt. Before I went, I kept thinking of the past and of my father and brother who had died long before her, and I felt very sad all the time. I thought of death—my own and of those I loved. I returned from Mount Sinai with a profound sense of peace. I am no longer afraid of death, and I feel connected to a greater sense of purpose and wisdom that is beyond human reckoning. I knew my mother, father, and brother were at peace, and I let go of the past. When I hold my tiny piece of Mount Sinai in my hand, I experience a calm that is both grounding and healing.

Chapter 20

UNITY IN DIVERSITY

— THE HANGING GARDENS OF HAIFA —

*"The tabernacle of unity hath been raised; regard ye not one another as strangers.
Ye are the fruits of one tree, and the leaves of one branch."*

—*Bahá'u'lláh*

SACRED SITE
THE HANGING GARDENS OF
HAIFA, MOUNT CARMEL, HAIFA,
ISRAEL, 32°49' N 34°59' E

CORRESPONDING CRYSTAL
MARBLE

Mount Carmel, the "Mountain of God," is sacred to three world faiths: Judaism, Christianity, and Islam. But the Baha'i religion has transformed the face of the mountain into a new wonder of the world: the Hanging Gardens of Haifa, now visited by more pilgrims than any other site in Israel.

* Haifa, Israel

What this site offers you

- Unity across nation, race, and gender lines
- Goodwill to all
- A long tradition of sanctity
- Peace and tranquility
- Awareness of life's beauty

Crystal Connections

Carmel is a volcanic Basalt mountain thrusting through marine sedimentary rocks—the entire area was once submerged in the sea. Much of the stone at Haifa comes from local sites. The white Marble of the monuments is from the source ancient Athenian carvers used: the Penteliko Mountains

The Hanging Gardens of Haifa

Founded a century and a half ago, the Baha'i faith believes that the Earth is one country with humankind as its citizens. The Hanging Gardens were built to reflect this worldview. They center around the Shrine of the Báb, where the founder was laid to rest on March 21, 1909.

The Báb's remains lie in a six-room mausoleum constructed from local stone. The golden dome over the mausoleum was completed in 1953, and a series of decorative garden terraces around the shrine was finished in 2001. The shrine features the sacred number nine, a symbol of the nine manifestations of God: Moses, Buddha, Zoroaster, Confucius, Jesus, Muhammad, Hare Krishna, the Báb, and Bahá'u'lláh. Followers of Baha'i are encouraged to make a pilgrimage to the site at least once. An important aspect of pilgrimage is to connect with other races, nations, and genders.

MYTHOLOGY, LEGENDS, AND LORE

In Canaan and early Judaism, high places were considered sacred because they were closer to God. In mainstream Jewish, Christian, and Islamic thought, Elijah is associated with the mountain. He lived in a grotto there and rebuilt an altar to Yahweh. Elijah challenged 450 prophets of Baal to a contest at the altar to light a sacrificial fire (I Kings 18). After the priests of Baal failed, fire fell from the sky at Elijah's command.

The metaphysician Iamblichus describes Pythagoras visiting the mountain on account of its sacredness, stating that it was the most holy of all mountains and that access was forbidden to many. The historian Tacitus tells us that an oracle abided here, whom the Emperor Vespasian consulted.

THE FOUNDERS

In the 1840s, a descendant of the prophet Muhammad began preaching in Persia. This young Shiite mystic took the title of Bab: the Gateway of Divine Perfection. He proclaimed himself a mahdi, a divinely sent

The Shrine of the Báb, Mount Carmel, and the Hanging Gardens: The Gateway of Divine Perfection

prophet who would release his people from oppression. Executed as a heretic in 1850, the Bab foretold a world teacher and one of his followers, Bahá'u'lláh, proclaimed himself the "promised one." Sent into exile, Bahá'u'lláh was imprisoned and died at Acre.

Bahá'u'lláh's son took the teachings worldwide. A core tenet says that all religions are manifestations of truth. Since that time, many Baha'is have been martyred for their faith, but the religion continues to grow and embrace all other beliefs into one community:

"Let your vision be world embracing . . . If the learned and worldly-wise men of this age were to allow mankind to inhale the fragrance of fellowship and love, every understanding heart would apprehend the meaning of true liberty, and discover the secret of undisturbed peace and absolute composure."

Bahá'u'lláh

St. George's Monastery and the Cave of Elijah.

Marble: The Soul Polisher

Marble has been extensively used to create the shrines at the Hanging Gardens. A Calcite that has undergone harsh transformation through enormous pressure, Marble accompanies you through soul-scouring challenges. It supports you during traumatic or energetic changes, stimulating your resilience and your survival instincts. This stone helps you recognize that you are an eternal being undergoing yet another transformation.

MARBLE'S PROPERTIES

This uncompromising stone insists you shake off lethargy and get on with life no matter what it might bring. Keep a piece of Marble in your pocket during changes as it strengthens courage during adversity and helps you ride out unavoidable traumas and conflicts with equanimity. This calming stone teaches that true security is found in your inner self. If your life is chaotic, Marble helps you find stability of purpose. With its assistance, you polish your soul to a shining brightness. Meditate with Marble to gain insight into the changes needed to bring hope and joy into your life. The stone also suggests coping strategies to help you through your present experience.

Marble

MARBLE'S HEALING POWER

Marble is a stress reducer that helps you recognize and deal with the underlying causes of dis-ease.

CONNECTING TO MARBLE

Marble helps you rise above challenges and conflicts to see the bigger picture. It takes you beyond petty divisions of race, creed, or gender into peace and expands a unity consciousness.

Rising Above

Marble connects you to the Hanging Gardens and the profoundly peaceful intention of this place. The stone helps you realize you are part of All That Is, fostering brotherhood with all of humanity and unity in plurality.

PREPARATION

Cleanse your stone and ensure that you will not be disturbed for fifteen minutes. Respectfully request permission to connect to this site. Light a candle and place it between you and the illustration of the Hanging Gardens terraces. Sit comfortably.

THE MEDITATION

Hold your stone at your heart and feel the energy strengthening and calming you. With half-closed eyes, look through the candle to the photo. Imagine yourself ascending the steps. As you climb, the challenges of your everyday life fall way; you become aware of joining with all humanity, rising above petty conflicts into pure, loving peace. As you approach the dome, know that you are one with everything. Sit, smell the flowers, breathe, and feel blessed.

When you are ready to leave, walk down the steps and bring your awareness back into the room. Put your stone down, but leave its peace in your heart. Go about your daily business in peace.

◀ The steps at Haifi lead you to increasing levels of peace.

Alternative Crystals

Smoky Quartz and Basalt are common in this region.

Smoky Quartz

Black Basalt

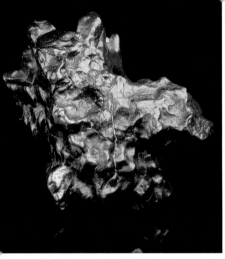
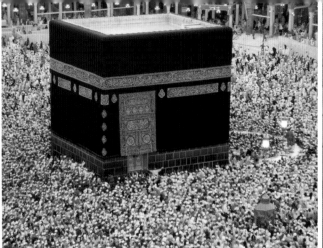

Chapter 21

THE FIRST HOUSE
OF GOD

— GRAND MOSQUE, MECCA —

*"The stone, when one kisses it, has a softness and freshness which delights the mouth,
so much so that he who places his lips upon it wishes never to remove them. It suffices, moreover,
that the prophet said that it is the Right Hand of God on Earth."*

— *Ibn Jubayr, twelfth-century geographer–poet*

SACRED SITE
THE KAABA GRAND MOSQUE,
MECCA, SAUDI ARABIA,
21°25' N 39°48' E

CORRESPONDING CRYSTAL
TEKTITE

The fifth pillar of the Islamic faith is that every able-bodied Muslim who can afford to do so must make at least one pilgrimage to Mecca. The site also has a long Jewish heritage, although Mecca is closed to all but followers of Muhammad. At the heart of Mecca lies the Kaaba, which houses an ancient black stone, a Meteorite or Tektite.

★ Mecca, Saudi Arabia

Crystal Connections

At the heart of Islam's holiest shrine, small pieces of black stone are embedded in the corner of a vast cube: the Kaaba. The stone was larger, but broke in the Middle Ages. No one is quite sure of the stone's origin. Polished smooth by the hands of millions of pilgrims, it is either a Meteorite—a totally extraterrestrial object—or a Tektite—a fusion of extraterrestrial rock and soil, created by a Meteorite slamming into the Earth millions of years ago.

Other stones form part of the Hajj ritual pilgrimage. In a golden cage stands the boulder upon which the Jewish patriarch Abraham reputedly stood, bearing the imprint of his foot. The pilgrimage ends below Mount Arafat. From the plains beneath, each pilgrim gathers forty-nine or seventy small stones and carries them to Mina. Here, three stone pillars symbolize devils who taunted Abraham. Over the next two days, the pilgrim throws the stones to symbolize a rejection of evil.

The First House of God: The Grand Mosque and the Kaaba

The Kaaba is much older than Islam, having been originally built by Abraham, the father of the Jewish nation. Abraham's son, Ishmael, is regarded as the patriarch of Islam. Muslims say Allah gave Abraham the stone when he built a shrine on the site, but, according to Jewish lore, the stone had first been given to Adam who built a temple there.

The eastern cornerstone marks the spot where Muhammad received the Quran. Every pilgrim entering the site contacts the silver-encased stone, revered because Muhammad touched it. Having been in several Islamic sacred sites including Kairouan, the fourth most holy, I have noticed that each site incorporates a similar stone. Great significance was attributed to Tektites in earlier times. Black stones were venerated throughout the ancient world and Meteorites were worshipped in pre-Islamic Arabia. In Cyprus, where the Prophet's aunt is buried under a Meteorite, the goddess Cybele was represented by a tapering black stone that now forms part of the tomb's cover.

The Kaaba has a tektite inserted in the front corner of the cube.

Some Muslims believe the Kaaba stone has supernatural powers. They say it was dazzling white when it fell to Earth during the time of Adam and Eve but turned black through absorbing the sins of the world.

Fire from Heaven: Tektite

Tektite is weathered and pitted, but it takes a polish and some Tektites are cut into gemstones. The stone at the Kaaba is either a Tektite or Meteorite. Both symbolize the alchemical fusion of "above" (the heavens) with "below" (Earth).

TEKTITE'S PROPERTIES
Due to its extraterrestrial origins, Tektite enhances communication with other worlds. It is believed that a Meteorite may have kick-started bacteriological life on Earth. In ancient times, such a stone was looked on as a gift from the gods. Plutarch referred to iron as the bones of the gods. Having passed through the heat of the Earth's atmosphere, Meteoric iron did not need smelting and could be worked "cold," so it was used millennia before terrestrial iron ore. The earliest iron artifacts date back 7,000 years.

Tektite encourages spiritual growth and assimilation of higher knowledge. It facilitates insight into the deeper cause of problems and helps you get to the heart of a matter. Tektite defuses volatile situations. Placed on the third eye, Tektite opens spiritual sight and telepathy. It is traditionally a talisman for fertility and creativity. If opposing or contradictory energies need to be harmonized, Tektite gently amalgamates the dualities into unity.

TEKTITE'S HEALING POWER
Tektite stabilizes the energy flow through the chakras. It strengthens the aura and balances male and female energies within the body.

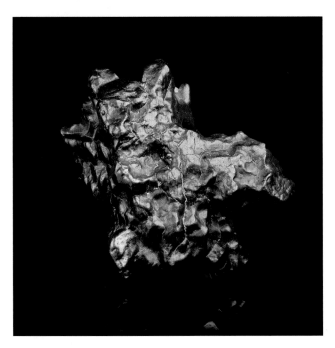

Tektite

THE MEDITATION

Sit comfortably, holding the stone in front of your navel. Exhale your breath into the stone. As you inhale, feel the energy of the stone coming into your belly. Become one with the stone.

Feel your awareness lifting and traveling with the stone, reversing the journey it made to Earth. (If you are holding an Arafat pebble, let it take you back to its home). You become aware that you are connecting with Mount Arafat and Mecca. Choose the time when you wish to experience this place and let the stone adjust time around you. Explore the energies of the sacred places as appropriate for you.

When you are ready to return, ask the Tektite to fly you back to your seat. Settle your awareness into your body. Picture a bubble of protection around you. When you have finished, put the stone down and consciously disconnect. Feel your connection to the Earth beneath your feet.

CONNECTING WITH TEKTITE

Tektite helps you contact extraterrestrial dimensions and offers you an experience of the divine. It takes you journeying to Islam or Judaism's holy places if this is your spiritual orientation.

Moving Time

Presently, Mecca is forbidden to all but followers of Islam. However, an armchair traveler is not limited by the boundaries of time or place. This meditation can be used to travel back in time to the ancient holy places of Judaism and Christianity. It connects Muslims to present-day Mecca. Or, Tektite takes you traveling to the stars, if you so desire.

PREPARATION

Ensure that you will not be disturbed for twenty minutes or so. Purify your Tektite. Respectfully request permission to connect to this site.

Alternative Stones

Any Tektite or Meteorite connects with this sacred site. Pebbles from the plains of Arafat are also appropriate.

Chapter 22

THE LUMINESCENT CRYSTAL MOUNTAIN

— MOUNT KAILASH —

"Only a man entirely free of sin can climb Kailash.
And he wouldn't have to actually scale the sheer walls of ice to do it—
he'd just turn himself into a bird and fly to the summit."

—*Garpon of Ngari*

SACRED SITE
MOUNT KAILASH, TIBET,
39°01' N 73°29' E

CORRESPONDING CRYSTAL
TIBETAN QUARTZ

*T*he crown chakra of the world, Mount Kailash, a mountain held sacred by one-fifth of the world's population and four major religions, is known as the "luminescent crystal." Climbing it is forbidden. A Spanish team had to abandon plans to scale the sacrosanct mountain after massive international protest. The base of the mountain is the world's most arduous pilgrimage route, and for millennia, people have circumnavigated it to purify their souls.

Pl. 67.

✳ The Himalayas and Tibet

What this site offers you

- Sacred pilgrimage
- Soul purification

Crystal Connections

According to the Hindu Vishnu Purana sutra, Mount Kailash has four crystal faces, one each of Ruby, Quartz, Gold, and Lapis Lazuli. Modern-day myth says there is a crystal city under the mountain. The mountain's bones are Tibetan Black Spot Quartz, but these are gathered away from the mountain itself.

Mount Kailash: The Precious Jewel of the Snows

Forming a "navel of the world" mandala, Kailash nestles in the center of six mountain ranges that create a sacred lotus. A natural pyramid, its four sheer, continually snowcapped sides face the cardinal points of the compass. The headwaters of four major sacred rivers flow off the mountain, dividing the surrounding land into quarters. Mount Kailash is the Jain, Buddhist, Hindu, and Bon "Abode of the Gods," deemed the source of all spiritual power. A single, arduous circumnavigation of this mountain purifies the soul of defilement and brings good fortune. Since the annexation of Tibet by China, access to the mountain has been strictly limited, so the opportunity for pilgrimage has been curtailed.

Pyramid-shaped Mount Kailash towers over the surrounding country.

MYTHOLOGY, LEGENDS, AND LORE

In Hinduism, Mount Kailash is the abode of Lord Shiva, destroyer and renewer, who sits in perpetual meditation with his wife and daughter. Tibetan Buddhists believe that Kailash is occupied by the Buddha of Supreme Bliss, Chakresamvara. Jains credit the founder of their faith, Rishabhadeva, with gaining enlightenment on the mountain.

In the *Ramayana*, Hanuman was sent to fetch medicinal herbs from the mythical Mount Kailash to revive Rama's dead fighters. Unable to recognize the herbs, Hanuman brought back the whole mountain. Once the herbs had been collected, he tossed the mountain back toward the Himalayas. It landed awkwardly and snow slid off into Tibet, forming the physical Mount Kailash.

In a legend that reflects the conflict between Bon, the indigenous religion of early Tibet, and Buddhism, Milarepa, a champion of incoming Buddhism, fought Naro Bon-chung, a Bon master. The two sorcerers indulged in a lengthy and terrifying battle, but neither was victorious. Eventually, they agreed that whoever reached the top of Mount Kailash first would be the winner. Naro Bon-chung flew toward the top on his magic drum while Milarepa quietly sat and meditated. As Naro neared the top, Milarepa passed him riding on the rays of the Sun. Surprised, Naro dropped his drum, which split in two. The marks can still be seen on the mountain. Magnanimous in victory, Milarepa flung a handful of snow at a nearby mountain, Bonri, and ceded it to the Bon religion.

MYTHOLOGICAL LANDSCAPE

According to the ancient Bon tradition, the spiritual realm of Tagzig Olmo Lung Ring lies in an area some scholars believe to be above Mount Kailash. Similar to the Buddhists' Shambala, it can be accessed only by those who have achieved purification and enlightenment. This beautiful, timeless realm experiences only peace and joy and has no duality.

Shaped like an eight-petaled lotus, or wheel, it is divided into four regions: the inner, middle, and outer, with a boundary around. At its heart is a pyramid-shaped mountain or axis mundi (world pillar). The four sides of the mountain face the cardinal points, and from the corners, rivers flow out of archetypal animals: the Narazara emerges from a snow lion in the east, the Gyim Shang from a peacock in the west, the Pakshi from a horse in the north, and the Sindhu from an elephant in the south.

Tibetan Quartz

Anchoring Spirit on Earth: Tibetan Quartz

Carrying the ancient, esoteric knowledge of Tibet, Tibetan Quartz has a centered, purifying energy that creates deep healing and metaphysical activation. The stone assists you in accessing the akashic record of past lives.

TIBETAN QUARTZ'S PROPERTIES

One of the most energetically vibrant crystals, Tibetan Quartz comes from high in the Himalayas. Holding the energy of the spiritual warrior, it deepens meditation and rapidly expands consciousness. Held over the third eye, it activates the chakra with the resonance of *OM*. This powerful centering and grounding crystal protects you while facilitating out-of-body journeying.

TIBETAN QUARTZ'S HEALING POWER

Buddhist medical texts consider Quartz one of the seven great precious substances. This master healer has an extremely powerful resonance. It aligns all the subtle spiritual bodies, imbuing them with divine light, and harmonizes the meridian and chakra systems. Tibetan Quartz crystals are often double terminated with

black spot inclusions. Double terminations break old patterns, so these crystals are excellent for helping you move forward.

Tibetan Quartz clears your aura and etheric blueprint, creating multidimensional cellular regeneration. It helps heal eating disorders and assists breaking out of dependent or codependent relationships that are causing psychosomatic dis-ease.

CONNECTING WITH TIBETAN QUARTZ

Tibetan Quartz takes you into the heart of this crystal mountain. It resonates with the whole Himalayan range.

Pilgrimage to the Sacred Mountain

This journey takes you into the cave deep beneath Mount Kailash to find enlightenment.

PREPARATION

Purify your crystal and respectfully request to access the secrets of the crystal mountain.

THE MEDITATION

Holding your crystal, gaze at the picture of the mountain. Feel the crystal's energy flying you high above the Himalayas, then placing you gently at the mountain's foot. Feel yourself walking around the sacred pilgrim route until you reach the crystal cave. Settle yourself comfortably in the cave and wait for enlightenment.

When you are ready to leave, continue your sacred perambulation around the mountain until you return to your starting point. Sense the crystal calling you back to your body. Feel your contact with it and the Earth.

Alternative Crystals

Nepalese Quartz, Himalayan Ice, Nirvana Quartz, Satyamani, and Satyaloka Quartz also access this sacred mountain.

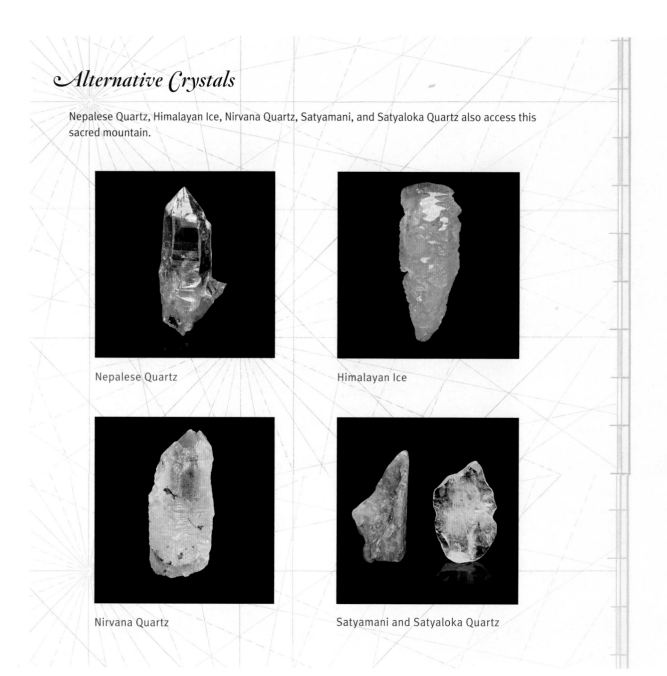

Nepalese Quartz

Himalayan Ice

Nirvana Quartz

Satyamani and Satyaloka Quartz

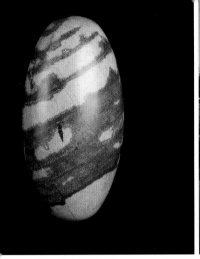

Chapter 23

WHERE SPIRITUALITY AND NATURE MEET

— THE NARMADA RIVER —

"To this Narmada, home to so many, religion to more, and beautiful river to all."
—*www.dharmakshetra.com*

SACRED SITE
THE NARMADA RIVER,
AMARKANTAK, MADHYA
PRADESH, INDIA 22°40' N
81°45' E

CORRESPONDING CRYSTAL
SHIVA LINGAM

*O*ne of the most holy rivers in India, Narmada is sacred to Hindus and Jains. It washes away sins and purifies the soul. Its bed is the source of Shiva Lingams, stones that symbolize fertility, destruction, and renewal. Thousands of devotees and tourists visit this site each year. Pilgrimages along the Narmada River take place under strict rules of humility, celibacy, poverty, and respect for the environment.

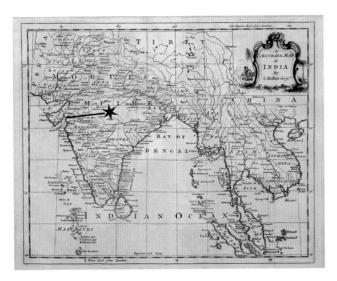

✱ The Narmada River crosses much of the Indian subcontinent.

What this site offers you

- Soul purification
- An immense source of creative power
- Chakra activation, energization, and balance
- Tantric union of male and female energies
- Access to the great cycles of life
- Deep and lasting peace

Crystal Connections

The Narmada is the source of the much-revered Shiva Lingam, emblem of the god Shiva. The rift valley through which the river flows passes through some of the oldest geological formations of India. A Basalt base is overlaid with bauxite (aluminum), laterite (rutile), schist, and gneiss. All stones from the riverbed high in the Maridhata Mountains—one of the seven great sites of India—are considered sacred. Microcrystalline

Quartz and Agate pebbles, and also Basalt, are naturally tumbled by the rushing waters. Most of the dual-colored Lingams sold in modern crystal shops, however, are artificially shaped Sandstone.

Legend says the goddess Parvati, Shiva's wife, fashioned the first Lingam from a handful of sand to worship the Lord Shiva. The sand represents the primal element of Earth and the Lingam shape the primeval power of the male god; the texture is the wise feminine goddess energy. A Lingam symbolizes the wisdom of the gods brought to Earth. A huge Jain temple of Bansipahadpur Pink Sandstone is currently being constructed, spreading over 4 acres (1.6 ha).

Holy Waters: The Narmada River

More than 620 miles (998 km) long, the Narmada is one of the oldest rivers: 150 million years. Narmada means "giver of pleasure" in Sanskrit, and the river is considered the mother and giver of peace. It is said that the mere sight of it cleanses your soul. Looking at it is as effective as one dip in the Ganga (Ganges) or seven in the Yumanu. Legend says, when the Ganga becomes too polluted, the mother goddess assumes the form of a black cow and bathes in the Narmada to purify herself.

The river rises at beautiful Amarkantak and passes through gorges, thickly forested mountains slopes, tumbling waterfalls, and whirling rapids. In the center of the river at Omkareshwar, a temple houses one of India's twelve great Shiva Lingams.

MYTHOLOGY, LEGENDS, AND LORE

More than 3,300 feet (1,000 m) high, the Basalt plateau on which Amarkantak sits is home to three rivers. Part of the ancient mythical kingdom of Kalinga, it houses three worlds: the celestial beings (gods and angels), asuras (demons), and saints and sages who achieved spiritual power here. Anyone who dies at Amarkantak automatically acquires a place in heaven. Amarkantak means "immortal obstruction" and, in the beginning, it was inhabited only by the gods. The town is at least 6,000 years old.

◀ The Narmada Tank, Amarkantak, source of the Narmada River

The Narmada River

Shiva is one of the major Hindu gods. Destroyer and renewer, he represents the cycles of life, death, and rebirth that govern all things. Legend says when Shiva battled another god over who had the greatest power, a Lingam appeared in the sky when Shiva was victorious.

According to myth, the river Narmada arose from the body of Shiva when he meditated so hard that sweat flowed from his body into a tank—still to be seen at Amarkantak. As the tank overflowed, it formed the sacred river.

The Power of Creation: Shiva Lingam

Shiva Lingam carries a powerful energetic charge. It represents ultimate creative power and the union of opposites, a nonduality that extends beyond the physical world. A Lingam is the cosmic egg from which all creation emerged and to which it will return as all things pass away.

SHIVA LINGAM'S PROPERTIES

God of mercy and compassion, Shiva protects a house from evil forces. A Lingam can be added to a household altar for protection and to attract love into your home. Some depictions of Shiva portray him as the "Lord who is half woman," showing that the power of the universe contains an equal measure of masculine and feminine energy. The bicolored Lingam represents male and female conjoining and the tantric union that merges the inner masculine and feminine energies into balance. This brings the body to a higher level of energetic resonance, creating a greater flow of life force. The Lingam also represents the kundalini rise that brings body and soul united into enlightenment.

A Lingam teaches "this too will pass." It releases you from the past and imprinted psychological patterns, particularly around sexual matters. The stone opens your creativity at every level.

SHIVA LINGAM'S HEALING POWER

A Lingam's healing power works through the reproductive organs and the body's electrical systems, stimulating potency and fertility. The stone gently overcomes

Shiva Lingam

Alternative Crystals

Basalt Shiva Lingams are also found in the Narmada and any pebbles from the river can be used.

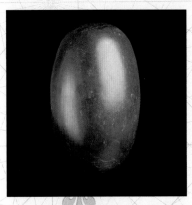

Black Basalt Shiva Lingam

memories of abuse and psychosomatic blockages. Placed over the uterus, it relieves menstrual cramps; over the phallus, it ameliorates impotency on any level.

CONNECTING WITH SHIVA LINGAM

Lingams are traditionally placed over each chakra in turn to activate energies and encourage enlightening kundalini power to rise up the spine.

Meeting Shiva

This journey takes you to meet the Lord Shiva, keeper of the cycles of life, and his female counterpart.

PREPARATION

Ensure you will not be disturbed. If possible, play or chant the Shiva mantra. Respectfully request permission to connect to this site.

THE MEDITATION

Hold your Shiva Lingam, close your eyes, and feel the power of the stone radiating into your body. Let the stone transport you to meet Lord Shiva.

Connection to the Shiva energy comes suddenly, as though you've been caught up in a great flame, or gradually as your breathing deepens. Greet the Lord Shiva and feel his power of destruction and renewal flowing through you. Feel how the two forces are equal and complementary, necessary for life.

Ask the energy of Shiva's female counterpart to join the process. Feel the energy spiral up your spine from the base chakra to the crown, uniting male and female, yin and yang in harmony, and then falling back to the base in a constant stream. Stay in this energy stream until you feel completely balanced around a calm center. Circle excess power into your dantien, just below your navel, to be drawn on as necessary.

When you are ready, thank the deities for their presence and put down the stone. Open your eyes, bring your awareness back into the room, and connect to the Earth beneath your feet.

Chapter 24

THE IMPERMANENCE OF BEING

— SPRING TEMPLE BUDDHA —

"Now, I, Vairocana Buddha am sitting atop a lotus pedestal; On a thousand flowers surrounding me are a thousand Sakyamuni Buddhas. Each flower supports a hundred million worlds; in each world a Sakyamuni Buddha appears. All are seated beneath a Bodhi-tree, all simultaneously attain Buddhahood. All these innumerable Buddhas have Vairocana as their original body."

—Brahma Net Sutra

SACRED SITE

SPRING TEMPLE BUDDHA, TIANRUI, LUSHAN COUNTY, CHINA, 33°77' N 112°45' E

CORRESPONDING CRYSTAL

CHINESE RED QUARTZ

The Buddha at Tianrui is the largest Vairocana Buddha and the tallest statue in the world. The Spring Buddha stands 420 feet (128 m) high above a lotus throne. Known as "He Who Is Like the Sun," the Vairocana represents the generative force of the cosmos. He creates and maintains the phenomenal world and his hand turns the wheel of Dharma. The figure is cast from copper but appears golden.

Sunrise over Lushan mountain

What this site offers you

- Connection to the eternally renewing cycles of life
- Buddha energy
- Purification of your karma

Crystal Connections

China's diverse geology contains many wonderful crystal formations, including numerous varieties of Quartz. Fluorite is common and creates beautiful Calligraphy Stone that assists in attuning to the wisdom of the past.

Spring Temple Budda

Paradoxically, the massive size and brilliance of Vairocana statues reminds us of the impermanence of being. The hill on which the statue stands is being reshaped to provide a fitting pedestal. The statue is placed above the Tianrui, an ancient hot spring famous for the curative powers of its 140°F (60°C) thermal waters. Nearby Foquan Temple, sited atop Dragon Head Peak, houses an enormous bronze bell used for sound healing.

Red Quartz

The Spring Buddha, Tianrui

The Purifying Flame: Chinese Red Quartz (Fire Quartz)

Chinese Red Quartz connects you to the energy of the Buddha and the purifying flame. It is one of the most powerful Hematite-included crystals. Red Quartz induces a feeling of being put through purifying flames to burn away karma, leaving the soul ready to start anew. This powerfully energizing stone fosters forgiveness. It teaches that apparent mistakes were learning situations that helped humankind grow in understanding and evolve.

CHINESE RED QUARTZ'S PROPERTIES

This Quartz promotes reconciliation and healing at a personal, family, or collective level. Easing the pain of genocide, it encourages forgiveness for the perpetrators. With this Quartz, you recognize that separation of the races is an illusion, all are connected in unity consciousness.

Red Quartz helps you to find the positive lessons and gifts in any situation. It highlights how an apparent lack in the external world leads you to develop a quality within yourself. Helping you to overcome despair, the stone restores physical vitality and helps you persevere,

no matter what obstacles you encounter. This is an abundance stone, beneficial for business and financial security.

CHINESE RED QUARTZ'S HEALING POWER

Red Quartz heals negative emotions such as rage, anger, and festering resentment that have a psychosomatic effect on the body. It supports oxygenation of the body's blood and organs, eases arthritic swelling and inflammation, and aids autoimmune diseases. In Earth healing, it stabilizes the planet, especially the oceans and mountains.

CONNECTING WITH CHINESE RED QUARTZ

Meditating with this stone helps purify your karma and allows you to start anew. It fosters forgiveness and helps you grow in understanding, stimulating your spiritual evolution.

Alternative Crystals

Any Quartz crystal is appropriate for the following exercise, as is Petalite or red-flash Ethiopian Opal.

Petalite

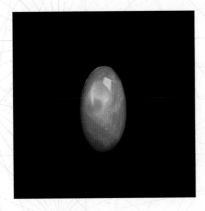

Red Ethiopian Opal

Burning Off Karma

This meditation helps burn away karma that you have outgrown, encouraging self-forgiveness and spiritual evolution.

PREPARATION

Cleanse your crystal. Ensure that you will not be disturbed. Respectfully request permission to connect to this site.

THE MEDITATION

Hold your crystal lightly. Close your eyes and breathe gently. Ask the stone to transport you to stand before the Buddha. Feel the stone growing hot in your hand until it becomes a purifying flame. Touch it to each of your chakras in turn to burn off your karma and purify your soul. End by gently massaging the past-life chakras behind each ear, working from left to right along the bony ridge at the base of your skull.

When you have finished, place the crystal in your lap and send forgiveness to your previous selves, who created the karma, and to anyone else involved. Disconnect from the crystal and picture a bubble of protection around you. Feel your connection to the ground. Cleanse your crystal thoroughly.

The Chakras

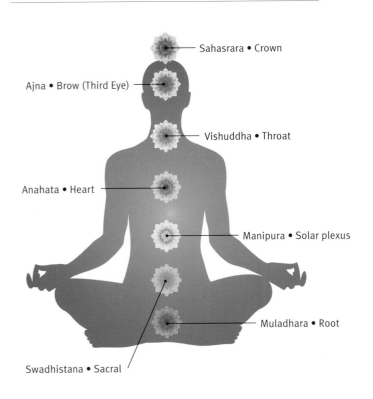

Sahasrara • Crown

Ajna • Brow (Third Eye)

Vishuddha • Throat

Anahata • Heart

Manipura • Solar plexus

Muladhara • Root

Swadhistana • Sacral

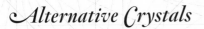

Chapter 25

HOME OF THE
SUN GODDESS

— ISE SHRINE —

"There is no place on this wide earth, Be it the vast expanse of ocean's waste,
Or peak of wildest mountain, sky-caressed, In which the ever-present power divine,
In even-force of nature's not a shrine."

— *Senge-Takazumi, Shinto priest and politician*

SACRED SITE
ISE SHRINE, HONSHU PENINSULA,
JAPAN 34°45' N 136°72' E

CORRESPONDING CRYSTAL
CHRYSANTHEMUM STONE

*I*se stands in an ancient forest of Japanese cypress, or Cryptomeria. In Japan, trees, stones, and rocks are objects of devotion, an expression of *mononoke*, supernatural forces that permeate matter and space. As such, rocks are regarded as *iwakura*, abodes of the gods. This profound reverence is the source of the rich spirituality of the rock gardens found in Zen and Shinto temples.

compressed into a matrix. Various other forms of Chrysanthemum Stone are found throughout the world, such as Celestite in Black Limestone. At Ise, pebbles and local rocks are also sanctified.

Ise Shrine Complex

Ise is more than 2,000 years old. The site spreads over several miles, incorporating various shrines and the Wedded Rocks with their view to distant Mount Fuji. This is a complex, interconnected site revered by followers of Shinto, Zen Buddhism, and other religions. Pilgrims are urged to journey here at least once—and almost 9 million a year do so, making it the most visited sacred shrine in Japan.

MYTHOLOGY, LEGENDS, AND LORE

According to Shinto legend, the spirit of Amaterasu, the Sun goddess—mythical ancestor of the imperial royal family and the highest deity in the Shinto pantheon—resides at Ise. Each year, the Japanese emperor attends special services at the innermost shrine, which only he can enter, to dedicate the new rice and pray for a rich harvest. Every twenty years, the main cedar-wood shrine is rebuilt and the spirit of the Sun goddess is moved to her new home. It was last rebuilt in 1993 at a cost of 59 million dollars.

✶ Ise, Japan

What this site offers you

- Ancestral connections
- Fulfillment of a traditional pilgrimage
- Connection to the Sun goddess
- Appreciation of nature in all its forms

Crystal Connections

Chrysanthemums, a symbol of longevity and death, are naturally depicted on Chrysanthemum Stone. The Chrysanthemum Stone found in Japan is Aragonite (or Calcite pseudomorph if the Aragonite has dissolved)

The Resting Place of the Sun Goddess: Ise Shrine

The home of Amaterasu, Ise's holiest Shrine.

MEOTO-IWA: THE WEDDED ROCKS, FUTAMINOURA BAY

The Wedded Rocks at Futami Okitama Shrine are lit in the early morning by the Sun rising over distant Mount Fuji, Japan's most sacred mountain. These rocks are regarded as deities. Tradition says one rock, Izanagi, is male and the other, Izanami, female. The two are linked by a cord, symbolizing matrimony. According to Shinto legends, the Japanese islands originate from this pair of rocks.

AMATERASU, THE SUN GODDESS

According to legend, Amaterasu was born just after the first islands of Japan were created. Shamed by her brother, she withdrew into a cave, which caused darkness to fall upon the land.

One of her sister goddesses reputedly danced lewdly in front of the cave to remind Amaterasu of her duties as the goddess of life and fertility. A face shining brightly in a mirror lured her from her cave: It was her own. Amaterasu gave her son three sacred treasures and sent him to rule Japan: a sword, jewels, and the mirror used in the dance. These treasures signify the Japanese emperor's unbroken divine right to rule. The mirror is kept in Ise's holiest shrine.

◀ The Wedded Rocks

SHINTO

Shinto, a nature religion, is the indigenous faith of Japan. Shinto's goal is to remove the veil that hides the divine nature of human beings. Shinto perceives healing and purifying power in mountains, streams, wind, and trees. The essence of life energy in natural phenomena is deified and worshipped as Kami. The four elements of worship are purification, offerings, prayer, and symbolic feasting.

Harmony and Change: Chrysanthemum Stone

A stone of abundance, Chrysanthemum Stone looks like a painted flower. As the chrysanthemum is the national symbol of Japan, this stone is deeply sacred. It is valued for its properties of inducing harmony and promoting unexpected opportunity.

CHRYSANTHEMUM STONE'S PROPERTIES

Chrysanthemum Stone centers you in the present, although it also facilitates time travel. This calm, confident stone helps you retain a childlike connection with the natural world. Teaching that spiritual development is joyful; it nonetheless insists that you progress

Chrysanthemum Stone

with your evolution and find your true self. Facilitating flowing with necessary change, it helps your endeavors come to fruition so you find stability and harmony. The stone is particularly useful if you need to see the bigger picture or are starting a new pathway.

Meditating with this stone helps you see where your beliefs and habitual thoughts block your progress and assists in identifying your true purpose in life. Chrysanthemum Stone is excellent for overcoming bigotry, ignorance, narrow mindedness, self-righteousness, and jealousy. By eliminating resentment and animosity, it encourages you to show more love to the world so that, by the law of attraction, more love flows into your life.

CHRYSANTHEMUM STONE'S HEALING POWER

Chrysanthemum Stone traditionally assists physical maturation, disperses toxins, and dissolves growths. It treats the skin, skeleton, and eyes.

Alternative Crystals

Aragonite with its profound Earth-healing properties is suitable for this connection.

Aragonite

CONNECTING WITH CHRYSANTHEMUM STONE

Chrysanthemum Stone helps you tune in to the profound peace and tranquility of the nature shrines in Japan and to listen to the direction of your own heart. Japanese society has been built on the concept of respect. Chrysanthemum Stone helps you appreciate that concept and build your own strength of character.

Connecting to Nature

Japanese religion honors nature in all its forms, and this meditation assists you in making a deep connection to nature. You can connect to the ancestors if you have Japanese blood in your lineage.

PREPARATION

Ensure that you will not be disturbed for fifteen minutes. Purify your stone. Respectfully request permission to connect to this site. This meditation is particularly potent if performed outdoors sitting against a tree or rock.

THE MEDITATION: MEETING NATURE

Hold your Chrysanthemum Stone in your palm and let your eyes travel around the stone. Marvel at how nature so cleverly portrays a flower in the stone. The petals look so real you reach out and touch them with the fingers of your other hand. Gently stroke the stone and ask it to connect you to nature in all its forms as well as the Ise shrine. Stay in the moment, feeling the connection. Don't force it; simply allow.

After fifteen minutes, put down your stone. Bring your attention back to yourself. Stand and feel your connection with the Earth beneath your feet.

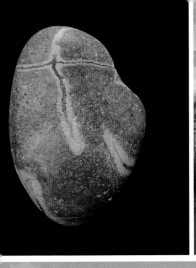

Chapter 26

THE HOLY STONE OF MOTHER EARTH

— ULURU AND KATA TJUTA —

"Aboriginal people can feel the energy and Light of Uluru even though they may live many miles from it . . . The depth of spiritual significance of this sacred site reaches into the very heart of all Aboriginal people."

—*www.gaiahealing.proboards.com*

SACRED SITES
ULURU AND KATA TJUTA,
NORTHERN TERRITORY,
AUSTRALIA, 25°20' S 131°01' E

CORRESPONDING CRYSTAL
ALCHERINGA STONE
(ULURU AMULET)

*U*luru, the mysterious red heart of a continent, has been sacred for at least 10,000 years but probably goes back into the mythical dreamtime. It is home to the spirits of the ancestors. Traditionally, when nomadic Aboriginal people moved to a new area, they buried a small piece of Uluru in the new land to keep them connected to Uluru and each other.

What these sites offer you

- Connection to the mythical dreamtime
- Ancient and enduring connection to the land
- Unity of purpose and people

Crystal Connections

The largest isolated rock in the world, Uluru is a massive Sandstone dome in the middle of a flat landscape. Like an iceberg, most of its bulk is hidden. A thousand feet (330 m) high, it stretches for more than 2 miles (3.2 km) and is more than 1.5 miles (2.4 km) wide. It penetrates several miles into the Earth. Scattered around the base of Uluru are small, trisected pebbles known as "Uluru's Children," Uluru Amulet Stones, or Alcheringa. The Aboriginal people have requested

that these stones no longer be collected for sale. Most amulet stones now available are a related type of Agate collected nearby or Mount Hay Thunder Stones. According to Aboriginal myth, the gods took all the colors of the rainbow and put it into Opal.

Uluru (Ayers Rock)

Solar plexus chakra of the world, Uluru is a powerful magnetic vortex point in the Australian landscape, connecting closely to the heart chakra at Glastonbury on the opposite side of the globe. Under different light conditions, the rock alternative glows bright red, blue, or violet. Known to white Australians as Ayers Rock, it was returned to the guardianship of the indigenous people in 1985 and reverted to its Aboriginal name, Uluru.

Its caves, pools, and gullies have long been places of ritual and ceremony. To the Aborigines, this stark mound is sacred ground, and it is sacrilege to climb it or to take stones away. For them, it is the heart of their land and they request that visitors respect its sacredness.

MYTHOLOGY, LEGENDS, AND LORE

Uluru is important in Aboriginal creation mythology, and the caves around its base carry pictographs of dreamtime stories. The Aboriginal people believe Uluru called them to Gonwana (Australia), and that this mound is where Balame, the divine father, meets Ngaya, the divine mother. According to myth, the bodies of the ancestors hardened into features on the ground. Various outcrops represent different spirits invoked by touching the rock. The birthing pool of the mythical Rainbow Serpent lies at the rock's foot.

Myth says that during the dreamtime, the land existed but was formless. One legend says Uluru was created when two boys played with mud. In the dreamtime, huge ancestral beings wandered the Earth, fighting and performing sacred ceremonies. Where they traveled, the Earth took on form to commemorate their passing. During the dreamtime, laws and traditions were made that still govern Aboriginal life today. Each clan claims a kinship with one of these original beings, their totem animal.

Uluru and one of its Aboriginal guardians ▶

The red domes of Kata Tjuta

Kata Tjuta (The Olgas)

Part of the same national park, Kata Tjuta (The Olgas) also figures largely in Aboriginal spirituality. The name means "many heads" and thirty-six knobs of conglomerate rock are scattered over an area of 10 square miles (26 sq km). Kata Tjuta is a much less visited site than Uluru. This site is a mythological map tied together with song lines. Each dome represents an event from the dreamtime. By walking the lines and chanting, Aborigines connect back into that ancient past. Past and present become one.

Uluru's Children: Alcheringa Stone and Uluru Amulet Stone

As Alcheringa Stone is reserved for Aboriginal people, nearby Uluru Amulet Stone or Mount Hay Thunder Agate is substituted. True Alcheringa Stones are trisected, reflecting the harmonious relationship between nature, the Earth, and all creatures that live on it.

ULURU AMULET STONE'S PROPERTIES

Amulet stones are traditionally carried for protection and good luck, but Alcheringa Stones have a much deeper property: that of connection to the land, the spirit of the ancestors, and the dreamtime. The stone stores the energy of its volcanic origins, which is drawn upon for healing. It can also be energetically charged by a healer or shaman.

Alcheringa Stone gifted to author many years ago.

Uluru Amulet Stone cleanses the biomagnetic field and lets a psychic view the aura or receive messages. By enhancing the wearer's sense of harmony and balance, the stone increases positive vibrations and physical vitality. Wearing the stone prevents anger and rage.

ULURU AMULET STONE'S HEALING POWER

Uluru Amulet increases stamina and helps overall coherence of the body. It protects against depression and weather-related illnesses. This stone cleanses the blood and has a beneficial effect on the metabolism.

Journey into the Land's Heart

This journey takes you into the sacred heartland of Australia and into the power of landscape and place.

PREPARATION

Respectfully request permission to connect to this site. Playing a didgeridoo CD enhances this journey.

THE JOURNEY

Holding your stone, envision the great red bulk of Uluru. Let the stone take you on a journey around the sacred rock. Feel its power as you walk; feel its connection to the ancient dreamtime and the song lines of this ancient land. Feel the rock singing you home.

Alternative Crystals

Mount Hay Thunderstone, (also known as Thunder Agate) is permissible for non-Aboriginal use, and Mookaite Jasper and Opal have a profound connection to this land.

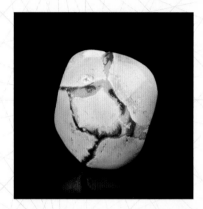

Mount Hay Thunder Agate

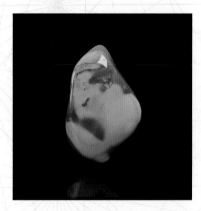

Mookaite Jasper

Opal

Chapter 27

THE POWER OF PLACE

— CASTLE HILL ROCKS —

"We are of the earth and the earth is of us. We are of the stars and the stars are of us . . .
Stone is the first ancestor. It holds the building blocks of life. Without stone we would not be.
It carries the story of the beginning of all and holds the seed of all that follows."

—*Barry Brailsford,* In Search of the Southern Serpent

SACRED SITE
CASTLE HILL ROCKS,
SOUTH ISLAND, NEW ZEALAND,
43°23' S 171°72' E

CORRESPONDING CRYSTAL
MAORI GREENSTONE (POUNAMU)

Castle Hill Rocks are part of an alpine basin containing an ancient "Earth university" predating the Maoris' arrival in the "Shaky Isles" (New Zealand). Here, you experience the true power of place. The land retains memories and emotions of all that has happened. The crystalline structure of the rocks holds imprinted information just as a silicon chip does today. It forms part of the cosmological lore of the Waitaha: a confederation of tribes from Oceania and the Americas who settled here to live in peace and harmony. The origin of Greenstone (Pounamu) working goes back to ancient China and tracks the migration trails of Polynesia.

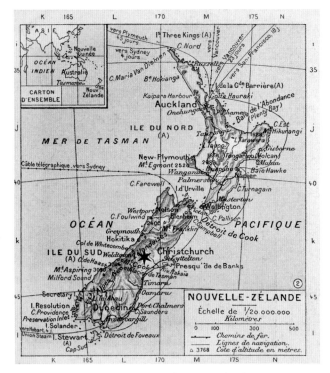

✳ Castle Hill Rocks, South Island, New Zealand

One of the teacher rocks at Castle Hill.

What this site offers you

- Profound connection to primal power of place
- Reawakening the most ancient sacred knowledge
- An understanding of the interaction of earthly and human intelligence
- A deep connection to ancient ancestral memories
- Strength in diversity
- Peace and unity with all humankind
- Aroha: love without bounds

Crystal Connections

Castle Hill Rocks are massive Limestone rocks eroded by the elements into fantastic shapes and simulacra. Although quite a distance from the rivers on the west coast where Greenstone is found, there is a huge energetic connection between this site and the sacred stone that traveled all over New Zealand and Oceania with its original keepers.

Castle Hill Rocks: The Ancient Universe

According to Brailsford, the Waitaha set up a center of learning that shared their lore, cosmology, creation stories, and navigation traditions—and stored it in the very stones. At this site, seven "staging stones" mark the stages of initiation for graduates of the old lore. At the summit, ultimate awareness was attained. This ability to shift perception into expanded awareness, Brailsford believes, enabled the ancestors to first travel in their spirit minds, and then to make the journey on land and sea, propelling cultural evolution. Ethno-

Castle Hill Rocks: Birthplace of the Gods.

graphic research shows that even before the Waitaha arrived, people had been traveling to these islands for thousands of years to collect Pounamu.

THE WAITAHA

"If we are not gentle with life, the garden within us dies."

Barry Brailsford, geomancer

The Waitaha traveled to the south island of New Zealand from all around the Pacific in search of magical Greenstone. These people could navigate for thousands of miles across vast trackless oceans using their knowledge of the stars and meteorological lore passed from generation to generation. The tohunga, their wisdom keepers, guided the great canoes that carried up to 175 people at a time. The Waitaha were not one tribe but many who came together to form a nation.

Tradition says the first canoe to arrive carried small, white-skinned navigators with red or blond hair; tall, dark-skinned gardeners; and olive-skinned, dark-haired people with a double fold over their eyelids who were of "the mountains and the stone." The people were specially chosen for the gifts they brought to the emerging nation, and the settlements were continually augmented by new arrivals. Eventually, more than 200 tribes settled here. Although the people worshipped Rongo-marae-roa, the peacemaker, they erected no sacred buildings—he was held within each person's heart and in the land itself.

It's said that after remaining on the island for a millennium without weapons, the Waitaha allowed themselves to be killed when warrior people intent on colonization arrived. The families gathered together, held hands to form a circle of peace, and awaited the deathblow. But the lore of these lost people remains embedded in the land and in the minds of the few elders who remain.

The Waitaha Creation Story

*"In the beginning the Earth and Sky were
one. Rangi, the Sky Father, was so much
in love with Papatuanuka, the Earth
Mother, that he held her so close the light of
the sun could not get in. Held within this
embrace were their seven children. There
they were kept safe in darkness so deep they
knew nothing of colour or light. Then came
the day when Rangi stirred, shifting and
turning just enough to allow Tane to catch
his first glimpse of the miracle that is light.
Stunned by all he had seen, he persuaded
his brothers to try to thrust their parents
aside to let in the light . . . None know how
long he took to open the way for the first
rays of light. But all concur that light gave
birth to energies that fostered huge strength
and life . . . The beautiful rains that fall to
water the planet are the Sky Father's tears,
a gift born of grief for all that had been
but was now lost. And the dews that form
on the grass in the cool of the night are the
tears the Earth Mother sheds when she sees
her lost love in the stars."*

Barry Brailsford,
In Search of the Southern Serpent

Greenstone

A Stone Born of Stars:
Maori Greenstone (Pounamu)

Found around a river mouth on the west side of South
Island, Aotearoa, Greenstone is a symbol of peace and
healing, revered by Maori people and the Waitaha who
came before them. Since 1997, it has been under Maori
management. As a sacred stone, it must be treated with
the utmost respect. Ancient lore says that, given and received with love, it assumes the spirit of those who wear
it and acts as a link between giver and receiver. When it
passes down through a family, it carries the spirit of the
ancestors. Owning one is a profound privilege.

GREENSTONE'S PROPERTIES

Greenstone is Nephrite Jade in several colors including
green and white. When polished it has a waxy luster.
Beautiful Flower Jade or Marsden Stone, *Kahurangi*, is a
clear, light-green stone with feathery, cloud-like white,
orange, and brown markings. *Inanga* is a pearly grayish-

white stone that looks like fish skin. Medium to dark green with black inclusions, *Kawa Kawa* resembles a leaf of the pepper tree. *Tangiwai* is a bluish or olive-green transparent Serpentine. Its name comes from a myth about the petrification of a weeping woman. Jade workings have been found in China dating from 8000 BCE, and it is believed that lapidary skill moved south to New Zealand from there.

Greenstone was born out of the upheavals that created this plutonic land. The mother lode is soft enough to cut with a fingernail, but it has been compressed in volcanic fault lines under enormous pressure. The individual crystals interlock to become an incredibly hard stone that today is cut with a diamond saw. Its strength supports you during difficult times.

Greenstone plays an important part in Maori culture. When a Maori wanted to make an amulet, he sought a shaman's help to receive messages from departed spirits who directed him to the right stone. This precious stone is imbued with mana, spiritual power, and has many myths associated with it. For more than 1,000 years it was carried across the arduous Greenstone Mountain Trail to the east coast. Traditionally, it is gifted rather than purchased and beautiful carved hei-tiki, Pounama neck pendants, are highly prized. Each shape has a symbolic meaning and a magical, ritual purpose.

Stimulating metaphysical abilities, Greenstone holds memories of the past and knowledge of the future. It receives messages and passes them to its keeper.

GREENSTONE'S HEALING POWER
A calming stone, Greenstone is a master healer, a stone of long life and immense power. It resonates with the kidneys and eyes.

CONNECTING WITH GREENSTONE
The Maori and Waitaha polished Greenstone by rubbing it against their faces or working it with their hands. Not only does this increase the luster, it connects you to the spirit of the stone and the knowledge that it holds within its translucent depths.

Alternative Crystals

Any type of Jade or native New Zealand stone makes this connection.

Jade

Amulet fashioned out of Pounamu (Maori Greenstone).

The Greenstone Meditation

This meditation takes you deep into the ancient past to connect to a time when nature, humankind, and the divine were one, linked in unity consciousness.

PREPARATION

Sit quietly, holding your Greenstone, and gently work it with your hands or rub it against your face. Move it in a circular motion lightly over your third eye to stimulate imagery. Respectfully request permission to connect to this site. When your stone is warm, begin the meditation.

THE MEDITATION

Hold your Greenstone gently and mentally communicate with its spirit. Respectfully ask to be connected to the knowledge of the distant past, to become one with the Earth and all that is upon, within, and above it ...

When the meditation is complete, put the stone aside, either on an altar or wrapped in a cloth until you meditate with it again. Or, wear it constantly to remind you of your journey.

Ba's Story, from Hamish Miller's *In Search of the Southern Serpent*

"Ba [was] somehow aware that something special was about to happen. She told me later that a young, dignified Maori man, carrying a long staff, appeared suddenly from somewhere amongst the rocks, walked towards Hine Aorangi and gave her a ceremonial greeting. As he sat down beside her Hine Aorangi carefully took a large polished pounamu . . . from her backpack. They sang quietly together for a few minutes then she rose alone to walk carefully towards the centre, stood very still, and then gently used her foot to move the small stone I'd used to mark the energy point.

"Ba was riveted by what Hine Aorangi was doing. There was no way this young woman could possibly know that it had been deliberately put there earlier to indicate the power centre. Placing the Greenstone on the spot, she stepped back with head raised to the sky and sang a soft Maori song to the universe . . . By gesture she invited Ba and three other females . . . to join her at the centre. They sang her song with her, all five joining in an embrace honouring the sanctity of the place and the earth mother. Ba was deeply moved by the simple ceremony, felt very privileged to be present, and to this day savours the experience."

Chapter 28

THE WOMB OF RE-CREATION

— KILAUEA VOLCANO —

"The re-creation of the world in miniature in a timeframe we can witness."
—*David Eastoe, plant-spirit essence maker, musician, and workshop facilitator*

SACRED SITE
KILAUEA VOLCANO,
BIG ISLAND, HAWAII,
19°25' N 155°17' W

CORRESPONDING CRYSTAL
LAVA STONE WITH OLIVINE

*H*awaii sits in an ocean 2,000 miles (3,219 km) from any mainland, and some people believe it is the tip of the long-lost continent Lemuria. This ancient continent still exists in a subtle etheric form and is being re-created by volcanic activity. The world's most active volcano, Mount Kilauea, is on Big Island, and the fire goddess Pele lives in the volcano's central crater.

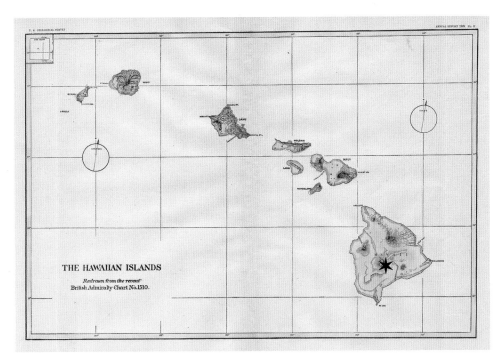

* Big Island, Hawaii and the Hawaiian archepelego

What this site offers you

- Re-creation and renewal
- Connection with the awesome power of the Earth
- Safely traversing the abyss
- Heart centeredness

Crystal Connections

The main rock on Hawaii is volcanic Basalt with pieces of Olivine created in the magma chamber. Small pieces are found on the slopes of the volcano, but visitors are warned not to take them home. The national park rangers constantly receive stones in the mail, which people return because they believe the stones have brought misfortune. However, Peridot, energetically similar to Olivine, or Basalt from other regions connects to the site.

Kilauea Volcano: Big Island, Hawaii

Big Island is like an iceberg with only the tip above the surface. The bulk of the island goes deep down into the sea, giving direct access to the molten core of the Earth. The ash and lava are highly fertile. Nearby, there is a yoni cave with a huge lava bubble sitting on a suspended ceiling. The cave symbolizes the feminine process of fertilization and creation with the "male" cone of the volcano above.

Traditionally, Pele appears to signal a new lava flow and local people make offerings to appease her. Although the goddess has been enthusiastically embraced by the New Age, the indigenous people are uncomfortable with nonnatives making offerings, and the island must be treated with respect. Hawaii is full of spirits who talk to you on the beaches and who underlie the island's heart centeredness. The whole island draws you into a potent relationship and helps you manifest what you most desire.

MYTHOLOGY, LEGENDS, AND LORE

Red haired and fiery tempered, Pele was born far from Hawaii. Her uncle, Lonomakua, keeper of the flame, taught her the secrets of fire. She was turned away from her home by her sister, Namaka, goddess of water, who feared that the island would burn if she stayed. With her companions, Pele journeyed to Hawaii where she fought Ail'au, the forest eater, for possession of the volcano. Today, Pele appears either in the guise of a beautiful red-haired young woman or an old hag, usually dressed in red.

According to legend, the ancient Polynesian god, Maui, captured the Sun as it passed through the zenith above Haleakala Crater. Maui demanded a special blessing for the Earth as the Sun reached the zenith each day above Haleakala—a blessing still given by indigenous people today.

The fire element vortex of the world.

HUNA

An American named Max Freedom Long claimed to have learned a secret tradition from friends while teaching in Hawaii during the early twentieth century. He called it Huna, from the word kahuna meaning "priest." Today, Huna is a thriving religion among New

The Four Elemental Vortices

The Earth has key elemental vortices that spin huge currents of Earth energy around the globe. Above the equator, the lines are yang (masculine/active), and below the equator, the lines are yin (feminine/receptive). These elemental vortices have been identified by Robert Coon (www.librarising.com/esoterica/earthchakras.html).

Element	Place	Quality	Property
Earth	Table Mountain, Capetown, South Africa	Yin	Light
Air	Mount of Olives, Jerusalem, Israel	Yang	Eternity
Fire	Haleakala Crater, Hawaii	Yang	Freedom
Water	Lake Rotopounamu, New Zealand	Yin	Compassion

Agers. Huna means "secret" and refers to the wisdom teachings of Polynesia. Huna divides experience into four levels of reality: scientific (objective), psychic (subjective), symbolic (shamanic), and mystical (holistic). Shamans (kupuas) learn to travel between these realities at will.

The religion proposes that each person has four "selves": a higher self that inspires, a conscious self that imagines, a subconscious self that remembers, and a core self that wills. The seven Huna principles are

- The world is what you think it is.

- There are no limits.

- Energy flows where attention goes.

- Now is the moment of power.

- To love is to be happy.

- All power comes from within.

- Effectiveness is the measure of truth.

This Olivine in lava was picked up from the beach thirty-five years ago with permission from the spirits of the island.

Olivine: Letting Go of Your Baggage

A powerfully protective and cleansing stone, Olivine is traditionally an amulet to keep evil spirits at bay. An excellent stone for detoxification, it aids letting go on all levels so you access a new vibration.

OLIVINE'S PROPERTIES

Olivine helps you release toxins physically, mentally, and emotionally. It opens, cleanses, and activates the heart and solar plexus chakras so you release "old baggage" from any lifetime. It clears burdens, jealousy, guilt, obsessions, and negative patterns. Showing you how to detach from external influences and tune in to your higher guidance, Olivine facilitates awareness that holding on to people or the past is counterproductive.

The stone helps you forgive others and yourself. With Olivine's assistance, you admit mistakes, let go, and move on. It helps you take responsibility for your own life, especially if you believe your problems are someone else's fault. With this stone, you make rapid progress in your spiritual evolution and understand your spiritual destiny. It is particularly useful to healers.

Pele's cauldron

Olivine in matrix

Alternative Crystals

Peridot, a form of Olivine, connects to Hawaii as does lava from other volcanoes.

Peridot

OLIVINE'S HEALING POWER

Olivine's tonic effect regenerates tissues and strengthens the eyes. Supporting the metabolism and benefiting the skin, it assists the heart, thymus, lungs, gallbladder, spleen, intestinal tract, and ulcers. Placed on the abdomen, it aids birth contractions.

CONNECTING WITH OLIVINE

Olivine connects you to the volcano and the awesome power of Pele. You experience the re-creation of a new continent and the immense creative forces that lie deep in the heart of our planet.

The Fire Ritual

This ritual helps you release baggage you have been carrying and lets you tune in to Pele's creative fire. It does not disturb the fiery goddess, which would be most unwise.

PREPARATION

Write down everything you choose to release, whatever baggage you've been carrying. Prepare a fire or use a candle and metal bucket. Find a red flower. Respectfully request permission to connect to this site. Do not invoke Pele; simply honor her in her island home.

THE RITUAL

Read your list. Offer the flower to Pele in honor of her creative spirit. Picture her volcano. Light the fire (or candle) and when it is blazing, put your "baggage" list in the flames. As it burns, feel the old energy being transmuted and returned to you as creative, regenerative energy flowing into your base and sacral chakras.

Pick up your stone and let the energy fill the stone— you can draw on it later as needed. Extinguish the fire or let it burn down. Thank Pele for her power of transmutation.

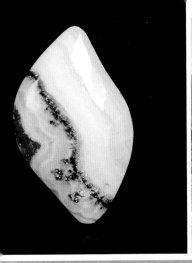

Chapter 29

A MYTHOLOGICAL LANDSCAPE

— MACHU PICCHU —

"There is a peace and an amazement that comes within a person when they first see Machu Picchu. There is nothing you can do to stop the emotions that begin to fill your body and your soul . . . Today I am filled with an inner peace I have never felt and I hope to carry it with me for the rest of my life."

—www.epianka.blogspot.com

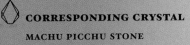 **SACRED SITE**

MACHU PICCHU, URUBAMBA
VALLEY, PERU, 13°09' S 72°32' W

CORRESPONDING CRYSTAL

MACHU PICCHU STONE

Perhaps the most iconic South American site—certainly the most visited—Machu Picchu has captured the public's imagination like no other. This mysterious and enigmatic Inca city was lost from sight for many centuries and does not give up its secrets easily. Its setting is extraordinarily beautiful, and it has been declared a UNESCO World Heritage site.

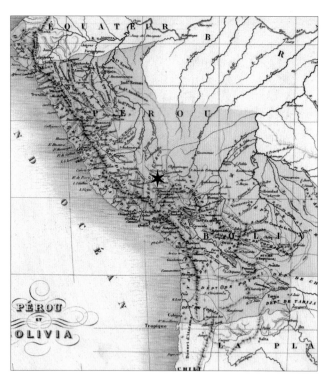

✴ Machu Picchu, Peru

What this site offers you

- Connection to ancient Inca knowledge
- A shamanic journeying route

Crystal Connections

Machu Picchu was built from local Granite quarried close to the site and is reputed to stand on a crystal cave that only shamans can enter. The central altar, called the Intihuatana Stone, or "Hitching Post of the Sun," is a sundial carved from living rock: a massive Granite plug. Legend says that touching your forehead to the Intihuatana Stone opens your vision into the spirit world. Other carved stones at the site can similarly be "read" by people with metaphysical abilities. Machu Picchu Stone, which looks like green Rhodochrosite, comes from the mountains nearby and connects you with sacred Inca energies.

Sacred Landscape: Machu Picchu

A world sacral chakra, Machu Picchu at 8,000 feet (2,438 m) sits in a high saddle between two mountains, both more than 20,000 feet (6,096 m) tall. Circled by mountains, it has a commanding view down two valleys and a virtually impassable mountain at its back. A sacred river, Urumbamba, runs in a horseshoe around the base of the mountain. The area is laced with natural energy grids. Local shamans say the whole area was a spiritual university for Inca knowledge, a numinous landscape in which the rock itself was imprinted with the mysteries—much as a computer would be today.

The Inca worshipped celestial beings and natural features in the landscape, and had extensive astronomical knowledge. At the center is an altar cut from a single 14-foot (4.3 m) block of Granite. The site includes an observatory and a sacred plaza where ceremonies and rituals were performed at the midwinter solstice to ensure the Sun's return. The Incas' ceremonial year started with the rising of the Sun on the summer solstice.

SACRED GEOGRAPHY

Giulio Magli, an Italian professor of archaeoastronomy, suggests that the whole area around Machu Picchu is a specially constructed ancient pilgrimage site. This mythological landscape lays out Incan cosmological beliefs and maps the Sun's path through the heavens. Pilgrims take a symbolic journey, treading in the footsteps of their ancestors.

> *"Machu Picchu was located at the ideal, opposite crossroads between the terrestrial and the celestial rivers. It was the other end of the sun's path."*
>
> Giulio Magli, *www.nationalgeographic.org*

City of Machu Picchu ▶

According to their mythology, the first Incas were created on the Island of the Sun on Lake Titicaca in Bolivia. After a harrowing journey underground, they emerged near the site of the present Peruvian capital, Cusco. At Machu Picchu, a disorderly heap of stones marks this void—Pacha-Mama, or Mother Earth, being associated with chaos.

The first Incas traveled a course that followed the Sun, and the layout of Machu Picchu follows the same path. The Milky Way had its terrestrial counterpart in the Urubamba River. Pilgrims left their ritual offerings near the entrance wall and numerous pebbles, mostly Obsidian, have been recovered here.

MYTHOLOGY, LEGENDS, AND LORE

The precipitous nature of Machu Picchu reflects the three vertical levels of Inca cosmology: Hanan Pacha, Kay Pacha, and Uku Pacha (heaven, hell, and Earth). These realms were interconnected through physical and spiritual elements. The snake, puma, and condor respectively are totemic representatives of the three levels. A shaman journeyed in trance through a vertical axis to the lower plane or Underworld or to the higher levels inhabited by the gods to inquire into the causes of misfortune on the Earth plane. After death, the souls of righteous individuals passed over a hair bridge to the higher realm. At the center of Inca religion and mythology was the worship of the Sun god Inti—the ancestral father of the Inca people—and the sky. The Incas associated Inti with gold, called "the sweat of the Sun," and honored him with magnificent gold artwork. The creator god, Viracocha, was known as the Old Man of the Sky and Lord Instructor of the World.

Machu Picchu Stone: A Landscape Captured in Stone

Machu Picchu Stone is so named because the colors and landscapes pictured on it resemble those of the site. The stone contains Cuprite, Manganese, Psilome-

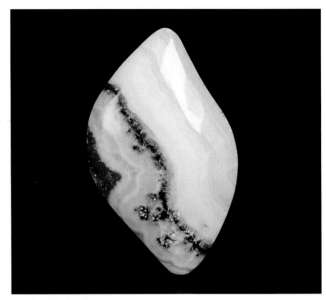

Machu Picchu Stone

lane (Merlinite), Calcite, Quartz, and other minerals. This beautiful stone helps you connect to ancient Inca knowledge.

MACHU PICCHU STONE'S PROPERTIES

Gentle Machu Picchu Stone connects you to powerful beings who want only your highest good. Use this shamanic journeying stone to visit the Incas and ancient cultures of Mesoamerica. If you were involved in sacrifices or cultural upheavals in former lives, the stone helps you to heal, de-energizing memories and restoring peace to your soul.

MACHU PICCHU STONE'S HEALING POWER

Machu Picchu Stone heals the soul and the subtle bodies rather than the physical body, but opens the heart.

CONNECTING WITH MACHU PICCHU STONE

Machu Picchu stone carries the intense energy of this ancient place. Journey with this stone into the cave that is the Inca heartland to experience the natural power of this amazing site. It opens your heart to the past and intensifies your connection with Mother Earth.

Alternative Crystals

Leopardskin Jasper, Rhodochrosite, Jade, and Obsidian are local to the mountains and have shamanic properties.

Leopardskin Jasper

Rhodochrosite

Obsidian

Journey to the City of Light

This journey takes you to the Hitching Post of the Sun and the crystal cave to experience Machu Picchu's power.

PREPARATION

Ensure that you will not be disturbed. Cleanse your stone. Respectfully request permission to connect to this site. South American music will enhance your experience.

THE JOURNEY

Breathe gently and settle yourself comfortably. Holding your stone, feel it lifting you and conveying you to the heart of Machu Picchu: the Hitching Post of the Sun. As you land, feel the power of the site pushing up through your feet.

When you are ready, walk down the ancient, sacred path to the crystal cave that lies at the heart of the mountain. The stone knows the way. When you reach the cave, sit comfortably, and listen to what the shamans of old have to tell you.

When you are ready to leave, walk out of the cave and ask the stone to take you back to your body. Settle comfortably back into your body. Breathe deeply. Wiggle your hands and feet to reconnect to the Earth.

The Hitching Post of the Sun.

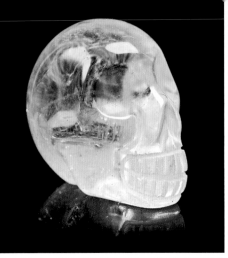

Chapter 30

HOLDING THE BALANCE OF THE UNIVERSE

— CHICHÉN ITZÁ —

*"Chichen Itza is an ideal destination, not only for those who enjoy archaeology,
but also for those who like history and the charming allure of ancient civilizations."*
— www.visitmexico.com

SACRED SITE
CHICHÉN ITZÁ, YUCATAN
PENINSULA, 20°41' N 88°34' W

CORRESPONDING CRYSTAL
CRYSTAL SKULLS

*V*oted one of the New Seven Wonders of the World, the serpent temple at Kukulcan, Chichén Itzá, honors the mystical powers of nature. One of Mexico's most-visited tourist sites, Chichén Itzá is complex. Little is known about its true use, although much is surmised. The Maya were an ancient civilization whose root races went back to before 5000 BCE. At Chichén Itzá, succession was through a sacred bloodline. They had a profound understanding of mathematics and astronomy and a sophisticated written language.

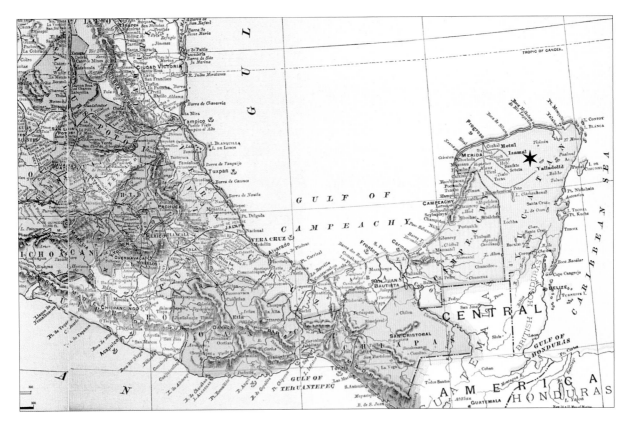

✴ Chichén Itzá, Yucatan Peninsula

What this site offers you

- Connection to ancient cosmological wisdom
- The awesome power of the gods
- Understanding the cycles of creation, spherical time, and multidimensionality

Crystal Connections

Many of the artifacts found here were decorated with Gold, Jade, Obsidian, and Turquoise, although no gemstones are mined near the site. Most carvings are in Andesite, a fine-grained volcanic rock from the region. Skulls are now available in many materials, but the earliest appear to have been of Quartz.

Chichén Itzá Temple Complex

Begun in CE 500, this temple was dedicated to the rain god Chac. Two deep pools, or cenotes, offered an enduring source of water in a drought-prone land. After the Maya abandoned Chichén Itzá, it was taken over by the Toltecs who introduced the cult of Quetzalcoatl, the feathered serpent. Jungle overtook the temples of Chichén Itzá and they slowly decayed until major archaeological excavations began in the 1920s. Since then, more and more is being revealed as the jungle is cut back.

THE MULTIDIMENSIONALITY OF TIME

Mayan creation mythology links the gods with the four cardinal directions, which were anchored by a central point: the World Tree around which cyclical time moved in a great circle. This spherical understanding of time and space gave rise to a complex ritual calendar. Rather than seeing time as a linear progression, the Maya focused on the cyclical links between nature,

The Pyramid of Kukulcan

The Wall of Skulls

humankind, and the cosmos. The solstices and equinoctial points of the solar cycle and the rising and setting of the Moon were celebrated.

Pyramid of Kukulcan

Perhaps the most famous of the Chichén Itzá temples is the huge 75-foot (22.9 m)–high Kukulcan pyramid dedicated to the feathered serpent god. Kukulcan played an important part in the Mayan calendar. Ceremonies there held the universe in balance. The architecture of Kukulcan is calendrically symbolic and still remarkably accurate today.

Each of the four stairways leading up to the central platform has ninety-one steps, totaling 364. When added to the central platform, this equals the 365 days of the solar year. On either side of each stairway are nine terraces—eighteen terraces on each face of the pyramid: the number of months in the Mayan solar calendar. Each terrace has fifty-two panels, representing the fifty-two-year cycle of the Mayan Calendar Round, when the solar and religious calendars realigned.

Carved serpents run down the sides of the northern staircase and are aligned so that on the spring and fall equinoxes the setting Sun casts a shadow onto the ramp of the northern stairway. The shadow forms a diamond pattern, like that on a snake's back. As the shadow lengthens, the snake slowly descends into the Earth.

Inside the pyramid, a much earlier temple incorporates a red-painted jaguar throne inlaid with Jade.

Tzompantli: Temple of the Skulls

In the temple of Tzompantli, rows of skulls are carved into a stone platform. Sacrifices were carried out at the site. After the victim's head was cut off, it was displayed impaled on a stake. At another temple nearby, a carving shows a human skull emerging from the head of a feathered serpent. The whole site sits atop an underground river. A nearby cenote (well) was used for sacrifices as well as offerings, especially of crystals. Early archaeologists retrieved enormous quantities of Jade and Gold here.

Cave of Balankanche

A naturally joined stalactite and stalagmite forms the central pillar at the Cave of Balankanche 2.5 miles (4 km) from the central site. Stalactites form when water drips through limestone, slowly depositing a coating that grows year by year. The central pillar is the World Tree, the anchor for the four directions. Offerings of incense were made here to the rain god in the appropriately damp atmosphere. In Mayan cosmology, caves were the entrances to the land of spirits. According to spiritual teacher Drunvalo Melchizedek, Balankanche is the heart of Mother Earth.

The World Tree, Cave of Balankanche

MYTHOLOGY, LEGENDS, AND LORE

The Maya believed four former ages or "suns" existed, each destroyed in turn by jaguars, fire, wind, and water. The present age came about when the feathered serpent god Quetzalcoatl made a new sun to restore life to Earth. Sacrifices at the site were intended to delay the destruction of this fifth sun.

The World Tree was the center pillar of Mayan cosmology, which understood the world to be arranged in three "worlds" watched over by gods representing the forces of nature. The Underworld was subdivided into nine planes ruled by Ah Puch, god of the dead. The upperworld, Earth, had thirteen levels. According to Gerald Benedict, author of *The Mayan Prophecies for 2012*, "the sky, a window in which the minds and activities of the star-associated gods could be observed was ruled by the Sun and [Moon]. Thus, the constellations, their seasonal movements and intersections were observable phenomena that also told a story about the gods."

THE MAYAN CALENDAR

The Maya used several calendars, none of which, according to Benedict, could "be understood without considering its relationships to the others. They interlock, they are interdependent, their combination providing important insights and perceptions that would be missed if left unsynchronized and considered only individually." The "short count" set out the yearly rituals and stellar events. The "long count" covered a more protracted period. Contrary to hyperbole and apocalyptic expectations, the end of the Mayan long calendar on the winter solstice in 2012 did not signal the end of the world, but rather the end of a specific period. A 5,126-year Great Cycle would be followed by a new cycle of creation, a cosmic shift in consciousness with huge evolutionary potential. Calendrical understanding was also aligned to the precession of the equinoxes, an even greater cycle of 25,500 years or so. This period was the time it took the spring equinoctial Sun to, apparently, process slowly backward across the zodiac until it reached the same point once again. The ancient Maya were uniquely aware of the cycles and loops of time.

MAYAN CHAKRA TEMPLES

Chichén Itzá is regarded as the heart chakra of a system of temples. In *Serpent of Light*, Drunvalo Melchizedek describes his quest to place a crystal in each of the eight chakra temples of Mesoamerica to realign and activate the female grid of the Earth.

Temple	Chakra	Quality
Uxmal	Base	new beginnings
Labna	Sacral	union of opposites
Kaba	Solar plexus	willpower
Chichén Itzá	Heart	unconditional love
Tulum	Throat	sound, manifestation
Kohunlich	Third eye	metaphysical abilities
Palenque	Crown	preparation for the next world
Tikal	Base	start of a new cycle

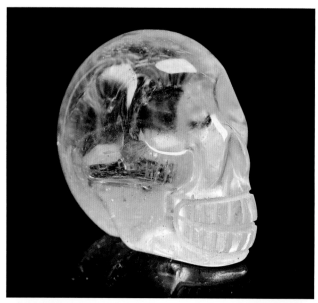

Mothers and Fathers of Wisdom: Crystal Skulls

"Crystal Skulls are the computers of the ancients, they contain important information that helps humanity to pass through its current series of challenges to take us into a Golden Age."

Unattributed modern shaman

Crystal Skulls come in all shapes, sizes, and stone types. They have taken on an aura of potency like no other crystal artifact. Believed to be 5,000 to 30,000 years old and remnants of the lost continents of Lemuria and Atlantis that possess magical powers, the ancient skulls reputedly were carved as receptacles for esoteric knowledge. These skulls, said to be inhabited by higher beings and extraterrestrials, are vehicles for profound teaching. Newer skulls are also making themselves known. They have created an energy network, like a crystal Internet, interconnecting them around the globe. They instantly convey you into the wisdom of Mesoamerica and advise us to honor Mother Earth.

THE LEGEND OF THE THIRTEEN SKULLS

According to Mesoamerican Indian myth, thirteen Crystal Skulls with movable jaws were carved each from a single piece of crystal. They belonged to the goddess of death. Known as "the mothers and fathers of wisdom," they taught that death was a doorway to another dimension. After death, the spirit rejoined the ancestors; the body decayed to fertilize Mother Earth.

These ancient skulls not only carried hidden wisdom but also gifts of telepathy and healing. Kept at different sites, each skull was guarded by appointed indigenous keepers. These ancient skulls are re-emerging to share their wisdom and assist in humanity's evolution.

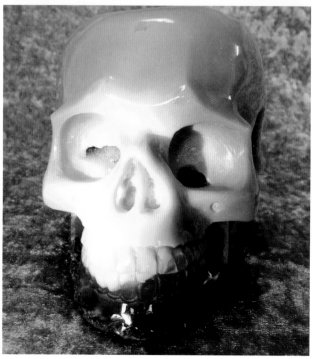

One of the author's Crystal Skulls (above, bottom): This one has a wicked sense of humor and abhors pretentiousness.

THE MITCHELL-HEDGES SKULL

One of the most controversial skulls—and the best known—was allegedly found by the late Anna Mitchell-Hedges at a dig in Central America conducted by her archaeologist father. Anna claimed that on her seventeenth birthday in April 1927, she discovered a crystal skull under a ruined altar. The skull lacked its lower jaw, which was later found nearby. Until her death, Anna maintained she had discovered the skull at Lubaantun: The Place of the Fallen Stones. However, evidence strongly suggests her father purchased the skull at an auction at Sothebys in London in 1943. Ancient or modern, once the skull was activated by people paying it attention, it took on a life of its own. It reputedly speaks, has a distinctive aura, and contains images of past, present, and future.

CRYSTAL SKULLS' HEALING POWER

To some extent, the healing properties of a skull depend on the crystal from which it is carved. Powerful healing tools for body, mind, and spirit in Lemuria and Atlantis, they continue to be so today.

CONNECTING WITH A CRYSTAL SKULL

Excellent aids for meditation and scrying, skulls are amazing tools for personal and planetary evolution—if used properly. Based on a long tradition of skulls that communicate wisdom and guidance to their shamanic keepers, all skulls, old or new, share a basic resonance.

Communicating with Your Crystal Skull

Place your hands on either side of the top of the skull. Gaze into its eyes. Ask that your vibrations attune to the skull. Ask the skull to communicate with you. Notice any thoughts or images that come to you immediately—or later in dreams or meditations.

Alternatively, if your skull is clear crystal, gaze into its back or into its eyes. Watch the images that form within it.

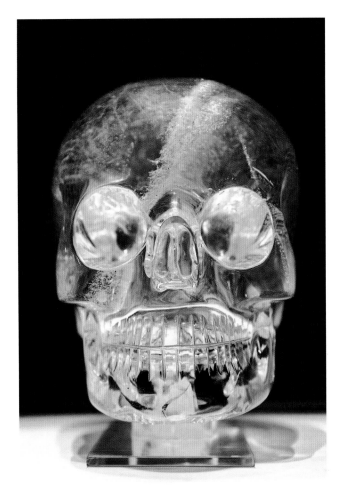

British Museum Crystal Skull

Judy's Experience: Entranced by a Skull

In 1976, I walked into a dimly lit room in the London Museum of Mankind. A Crystal Skull perched on a plinth suddenly glowed blue and pulled me toward it. I had no choice but to approach—it was like being reeled in by a tractor beam. I stood entranced, looking into the skull, observing life at a pyramidal temple. I thought I had spent a few moments watching the images form, but a guard tapped me on the shoulder and said they were closing shortly. I had been standing there for two hours!

Bibliography

Assmann, Jan, trans. Andrew Jenkins. *The Mind of Egypt*. (Cambridge, MA: Harvard University Press, 2003).

Bendict, Gerald. *The Mayan Prophecies for 2012*. (London: Watkins Publishing, 2008).

Brailsford, Barry. *Song of the Stone*. (Christchurch: Stoneprint Press, 2008).

Catlin, George. www.rocksandminerals.com/specimens/pipestone.htm and www.rocksandminerals.com/specimens/pipestonegeo.htm.

Coon, Robert. www.librarising.com/esoterica/earth-chakras.html and www.earthchakras.org.

Eastwood, Michael. *Crystal Oversoul Attunements: 44 Healing Cards and Book*. (Forres, Scotland: Findhorn Press, 2011).

Hall, Judy, *101 Power Crystals: The Ultimate Guide to Magical Crystals, Gems, and Stones for Healing and Transformation* (Fair Winds Press, USA, and Quarto, London)

Hall, Judy. *Torn Clouds*. (Alresford, England: O Books, 2001). (Now available as an e-book.)

Hallendy, Norman. *Tukiliit: The Stone People Who Live in the Wind*. (Fairbanks, AK: University of Alaska Press and Douglas & McIntyre, 2009).

Iyer, Pico, and others. *100 Journeys for the Spirit*. (London: Watkins Publishing, 2010).

Lilly, Simon and Sue, *Preseli Bluestone: Healing Stone of the Ancestors* (Devon: Tree Seer Publications)

Melchizedek, Drunvalo. *Serpent of Light: Beyond 2012*. (Newburyport, MA: Weiser Books, 2008).

Miller, Hamish, and Barry Brailsford. *In Search of the Southern Serpent: A Journey into the Power of Place*. (Christchurch: Stoneprint Press, 2008).

Miller, Joaquin, Malcolm Margolin, and Alan Rosenus. *Life Amongst the Modocs: Unwritten History*. (Berkeley, CA: Heyday Books, 1996, first published 1873).

Murphy, Anthony, and Richard Moore. *Island of the Setting Sun: In Search of Ireland's Ancient Astronomers*. (Dublin: The Liffey Press, 2007).

Murphy, Anthony. "The Ancient Astronomers of Newgrange," (lecture delivered to Astronomy Ireland, January 2002).

Phylos the Tibetan (Frederick Spencer Oliver). *A Dweller on Two Planets or the Dividing of the Way*. (Los Angeles: Baumgardt Publishing Co., 1905).

Robinson, Peter. *Bad Boy*. (New York: HarperCollins Publishers, 2010).

Shearing, Dr. Colin R. "Secrets of the Preseli Blue-stones," www.britannia.com/history/preseli_blue.html.

Snelling, John. *The Sacred Mountain: The Complete Guide to Tibet's Mount Kailas*. (London and The Hague: East–West Publications, 1990).

Sutphen, Dick. *Sedona: Psychic Energy Vortexes*. (Malibu, CA: Valley of the Sun Publishing, 1993).

Tyberonn, James, www.earth-keeper.com.

West, John Anthony. *Serpent in the Sky*. (New York: Harper & Row, 1979).

Wozencroft, Jon, and Paul Devereux, www.landscape-perception.com.

www.archnews.co.uk

www.bbc.co.uk/wales/arts

www.huna.org

www.innerpeacemusic.com

www.megalithic.co.uk

www.megalithomania.co.uk and www.megalithomania.com

www.psychogeology.com

www.world-mysteries.com

Resources

Crystals attuned by Judy Hall are available from www.angeladditions.co.uk.

David Eastoe's Petaltone Essences, www.petaltone.co.uk (crystal cleansers and reenergizers)

The Crystal Balance Co., www.crystalbalance.net (crystal cleansers and reenergizers)

Initiation by Steven Halpern is highly recommended. Recorded within the Great Pyramid, the chanting takes you into the heart of ancient Egypt.

Crystals, www.exquisitecrystals.com

Bluestone essence: www.greenmanshop.co.uk

About the Author

Judy Hall is a successful Mind Body Spirit author with forty-six books to her credit, including the million-selling *Crystal Bible* (Volumes 1 and 2) and *101 Power Crystals: The Ultimate Guide to Magical Crystals, Gems, and Stones for Healing and Transformation*. She has been entranced by sacred sites since childhood, and one of her earliest memories is of leaning out of her pram to touch a standing stone in a Welsh stone circle. Since then, she has visited literally hundreds of sacred sites ranging from the well known to ones way off the tourist trail. Judy has been a past life therapist and karmic astrologer for more than forty years. Her specialities are past life readings and regression, soul healing, reincarnation, astrology and psychology, divination and crystal lore. She recently appeared on the *Watkins Review* of the one hundred most spiritually influential authors of this century.

A trained healer and counselor, Judy has been psychic all her life and has a wide experience of many systems of divination and natural healing methods. Judy holds a B.Ed. in Religious Studies with an extensive knowledge of world religions and mythology and an M.A. in Cultural Astronomy and Astrology from Bath Spa University. Her mentor was Christine Hartley (Dion Fortune's metaphysical colleague and literary agent). Judy has conducted workshops around the world and has made fifteen visits to Egypt, the subject of her novel *Torn Clouds*. This book draws on Judy's master's research into the origins of sacred landscape and the worldviews that gave rise to such sites. See www.judyhall.co.uk and www.angeladditions.co.uk.

Acknowledgments

My deepest thanks and gratitude go to Page Amber Smith and her delightful daughter, Savannah, for the gift of Greenstone, something I will treasure forever. Gary Wallace was equally generous in sharing a small piece of Hawaii, given and received with due deference to Madam Pele.

With love and thanks to my daughter Jeni Campbell for the amazing photographs; a hidden talent has been revealed.

I am grateful to Dr. Colin Shearing, who has made a detailed scientific and metaphysical study of Preseli Bluestone and its connection to Stonehenge and who generously shares his knowledge, and to Chris Mitchell, who first introduced me to Preseli. Thanks go to the many guardians, guides, and keepers who have directed me to sacred sites and brought their crystal companions to my attention. I would particularly like to thank the speakers at Megalithomania Conferences who freely and enthusiastically shared their work. I learned from so many of you without you knowing it. Barry Brailsford was most generous in granting permission to draw on both his and the late Hamish Miller's work in their *Search for the Southern Serpent*. I would also like to thank Peter Robinson for permission to quote from *Bad Boy* and for confirming my intuition. Mike Eastwood of Aristia and Findhorn Press kindly granted permission to use the Lapis Lazuli mandala, and Watkins Books the Pico Iver and Gerald Benedict extracts. Gerry's book cut brilliantly through the hyperbole to the core of the Mayan belief system. Thanks to Robin Heath for help over many years with archaeological and megalithic infomation. www.skyeandlandscapes.com

My love and gratitude to the John Van Rees partnership (father and son). To John Snr. for the awesome crystals and to John Jnr. for this incredible photos that really capture the spirit of the crystals.

I am profoundly grateful to Skye Alexander for her sensitive shaping, to Betsy Gammons for her editing and picture research, which brilliantly enhanced the book, and to Jill Alexander and Will Kiester for their belief in this project. Blessings to you all.

Every effort has been made to contact the copyright holders of certain websites and various authors to obtain permission for quotations, but without complete success. Thanks are due to them all.

All crystals and stones photography by John Van Rees, Jnr., www.exquisitecrystals.com

AFP/Getty Images, 98 (middle & right); 100 (left)

© Arcaid Images / Alamy, 88

© Art Directors & TRIP / Alamy, 134 (right)

James P. Blair / Getty Images, 143 (middle); 144

Jennifer Campbell, 14; 24; 25; 28 (right); 32 (top, left); 75 (middle & right); 77; 79; 83 (middle)

Patrick Chapuis/Getty Images, 114

De Agostini/Getty Images, 72

Courtesy of Michael Eastwood, 21

Fotolia.com, 94 (right)

© Robert Fried / Alamy, 178 (right); 181

© Gallo Images / Alamy, 136

© Glow Images / Alamy, 180 (right)

Sylvain Grandadam / Getty Images, 153

Courtesy of Judy Hall, 182 (bottom)

Yoel Harel / Alamy, 131 (top)

Jim Henderson / Alamy, 116 (middle); 118 (left)

© imagebroker / Alamy, 178 (middle); 180 (left)

iStockphoto.com, 12; 17; 29; 35; 93; 95; 106; 109; 117; 143 (right); 146; 151 (right); 153 (top, left); 158; 163 (left); 168 (middle); 171 (left)

© Ei Katsumata—CMC / Alamy, 152 (right); 154

Christian Kober/Getty Images, 149

Robert Leanna, II, Illustration, 102

© Eddie Linssen / Alamy, 18; 78

© Lyroky / Alamy, 54 (middle & right); 60

Reinhard Marscha / Getty Images, 128 (middle)

© J. Marshall, Tribaleye Images / Alamy, 125 (right)

© Gunter Marx / Alamy, 28 (middle); 30

© Keith Morris / Alamy, 83 (right); 85

© nagelestock.com / Alamy, 157 (middle); 159

Courtesy of NASA/Wikipedia.org, 13

© PhotosDirect/Wayne Howes, 148 (middle); 150 (right)

© Prisma Bildagentur AG / Alamy, 152 (middle); 155 (top, left)

© Robert Harding Picture Library Ltd / Alamy, 11; 132

Robert Harding Productions/Getty Images, 103 (right)

Jochen Schlenker/Getty Images, 112

Shutterstock.com, 34 (middle & right); 36; 39; 41 (middle & right); 42; 43; 44; 48 (middle & right); 49; 50; 51 (left); 55; 62 (middle); 62 (right); 63; 65; 68 (middle & right); 69; 70; 71; 76; 84; 94 (middle); 97 (top); 99; 103 (middle); 104 (top); 108 (middle & right); 110; 121 (middle); 122; 124; 125 (left); 128 (right); 129; 130; 134 (middle); 135; 138 (middle); 139; 140; 145; 162 (middle); 163 (right); 164; 168 (right); 173 (middle); 174; 175; 179

Smithsonian American Art Museum, Washington, DC / Art Resource, NY, 58

Spectrum Photofile, 33

© David Wall / Alamy, 157 (right); 160

Courtesy of Wikimedia.org, Gerome Jean-Leon, 123

Courtesy of Wikipedia.org, 64; 100 (right); 104 (bottom); 116 (right); 119 (right); 121 (right); 138 (right); 148 (right); 162 (right); 166 (bottom); 169; 173 (right); 177 (bottom, right); 183

Index